TWO BECOME ONE

Best Wishes,

Brian.

TWO BECOME ONE

R. Lodge
and
B. Swinyard

Copyright © 2018 R. Lodge and B. Swinyard

The moral right of the author has been asserted.

Apart from any fair dealing for the purposes of research or private study, or criticism or review, as permitted under the Copyright, Designs and Patents Act 1988, this publication may only be reproduced, stored or transmitted, in any form or by any means, with the prior permission in writing of the publishers, or in the case of reprographic reproduction in accordance with the terms of licences issued by the Copyright Licensing Agency. Enquiries concerning reproduction outside those terms should be sent to the publishers.

Matador
9 Priory Business Park,
Wistow Road, Kibworth Beauchamp,
Leicestershire. LE8 0RX
Tel: 0116 279 2299
Email: books@troubador.co.uk
Web: www.troubador.co.uk/matador
Twitter: @matadorbooks

ISBN 978 1789015 720

British Library Cataloguing in Publication Data.
A catalogue record for this book is available from the British Library.

Printed and bound by CPI Group (UK) Ltd, Croydon, CR0 4YY
Typeset in 11pt Minion Pro by Troubador Publishing Ltd, Leicester, UK

Matador is an imprint of Troubador Publishing Ltd

For Angela and Francesca

Who simply rocked our worlds

We have two lives

- the one we learn with

- and the life we live after that

> Bernard Malamud

TWO

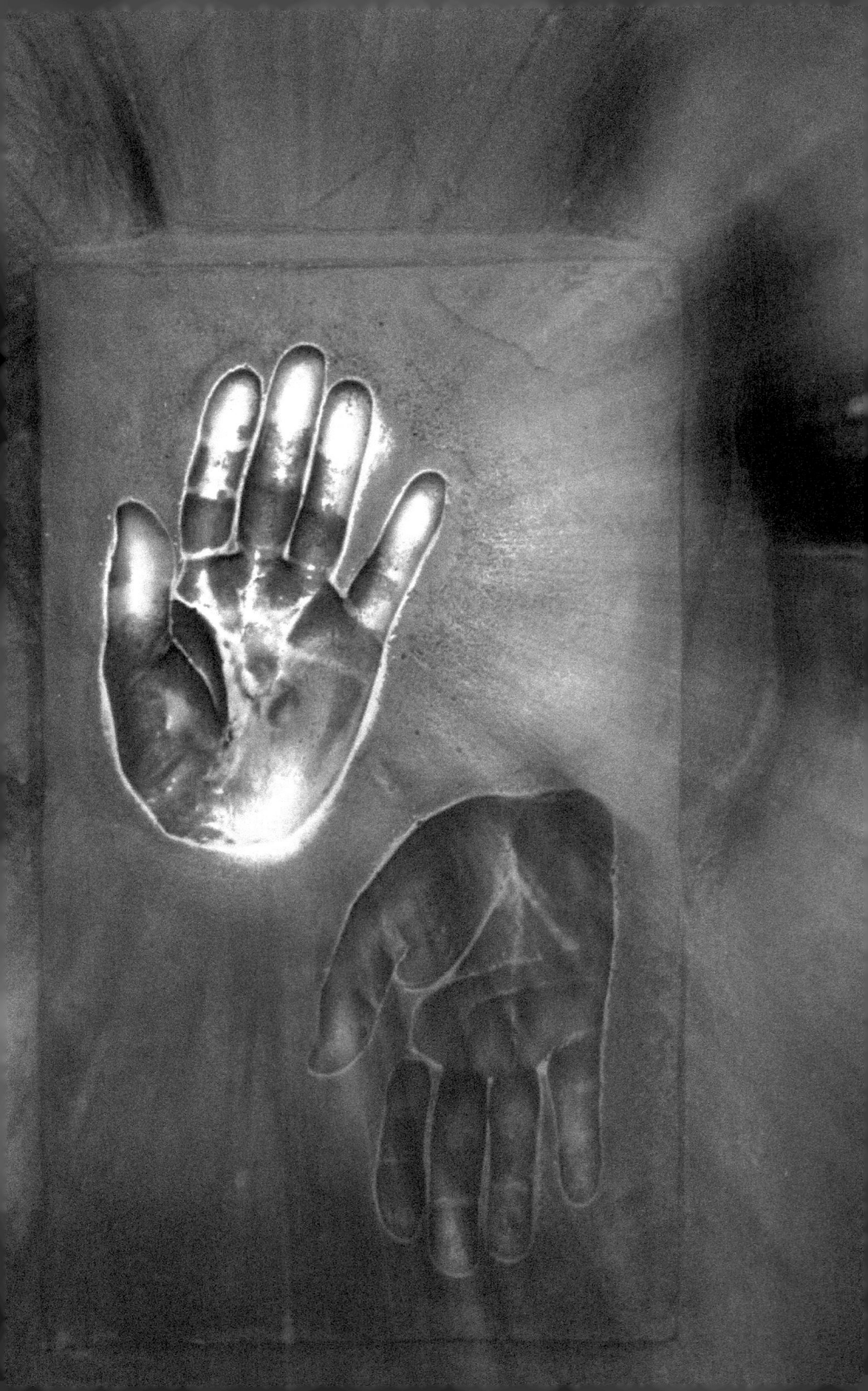

Open Your Heart

Take my hand
And I will
Show you the world

Open your heart
And I will
Show you eternity

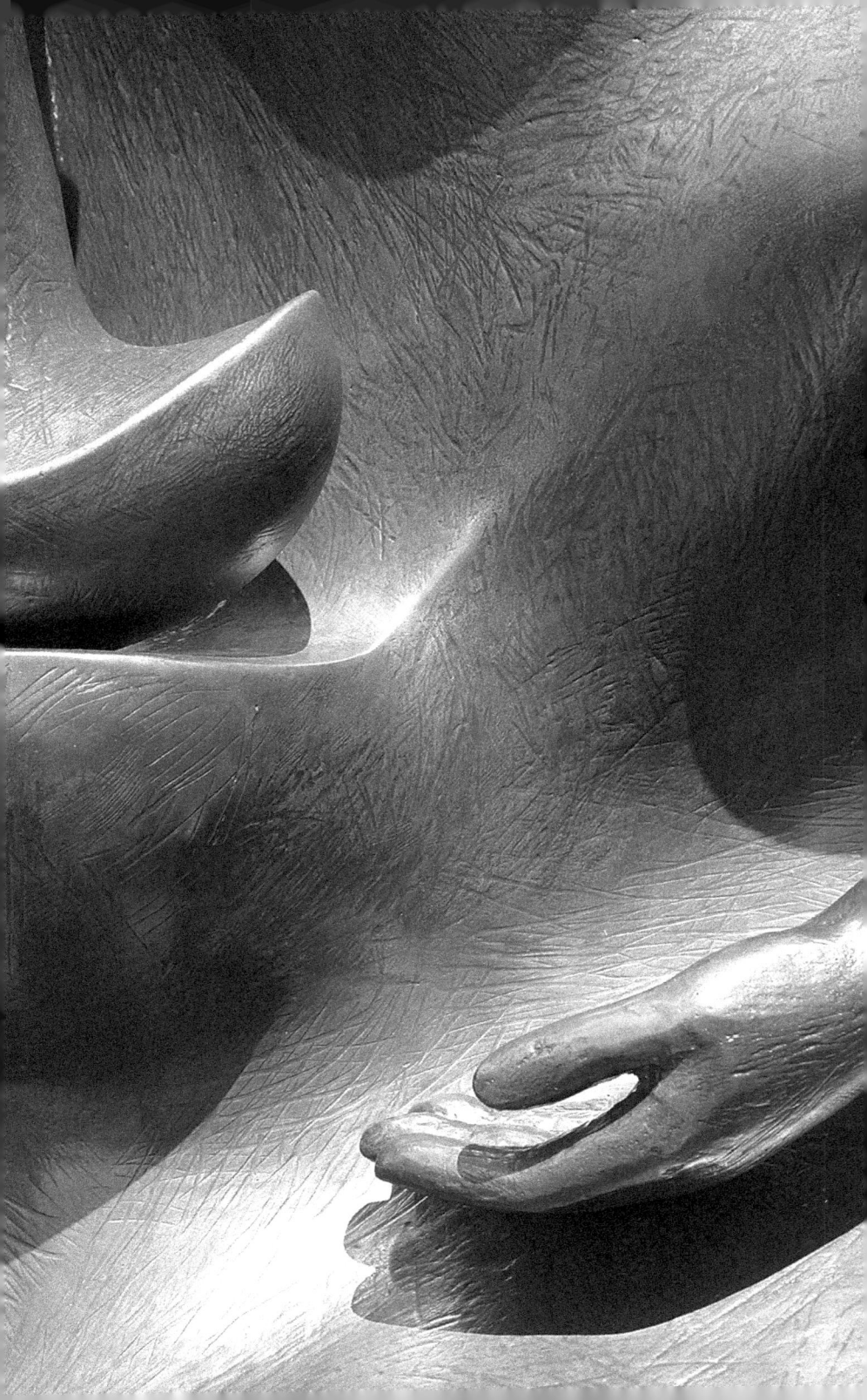

The One

Every life deserves
One great love
A single grand romance
Of utter abandon and freedom

One heart that beats
In divine harmony
One indivisible soul
Soaring in mutual ecstasy

One face etched indelibly
In memory unchanging
One name to hold on to
When all seems lost

And one hand to reach out to
When darkness comes

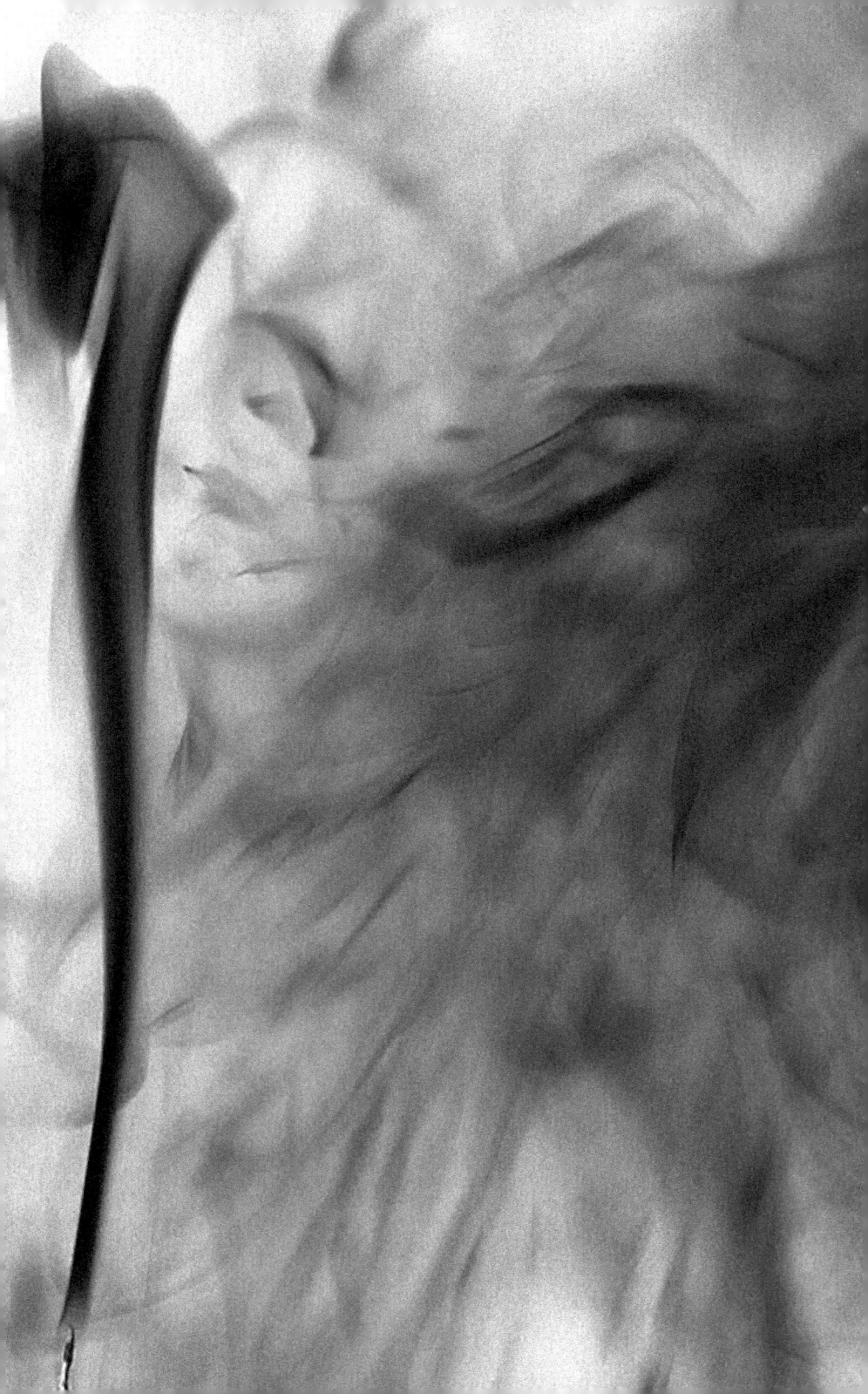

Uprooted

One glorious moment

In your arms

Uprooted me from myself

And I was lost forever

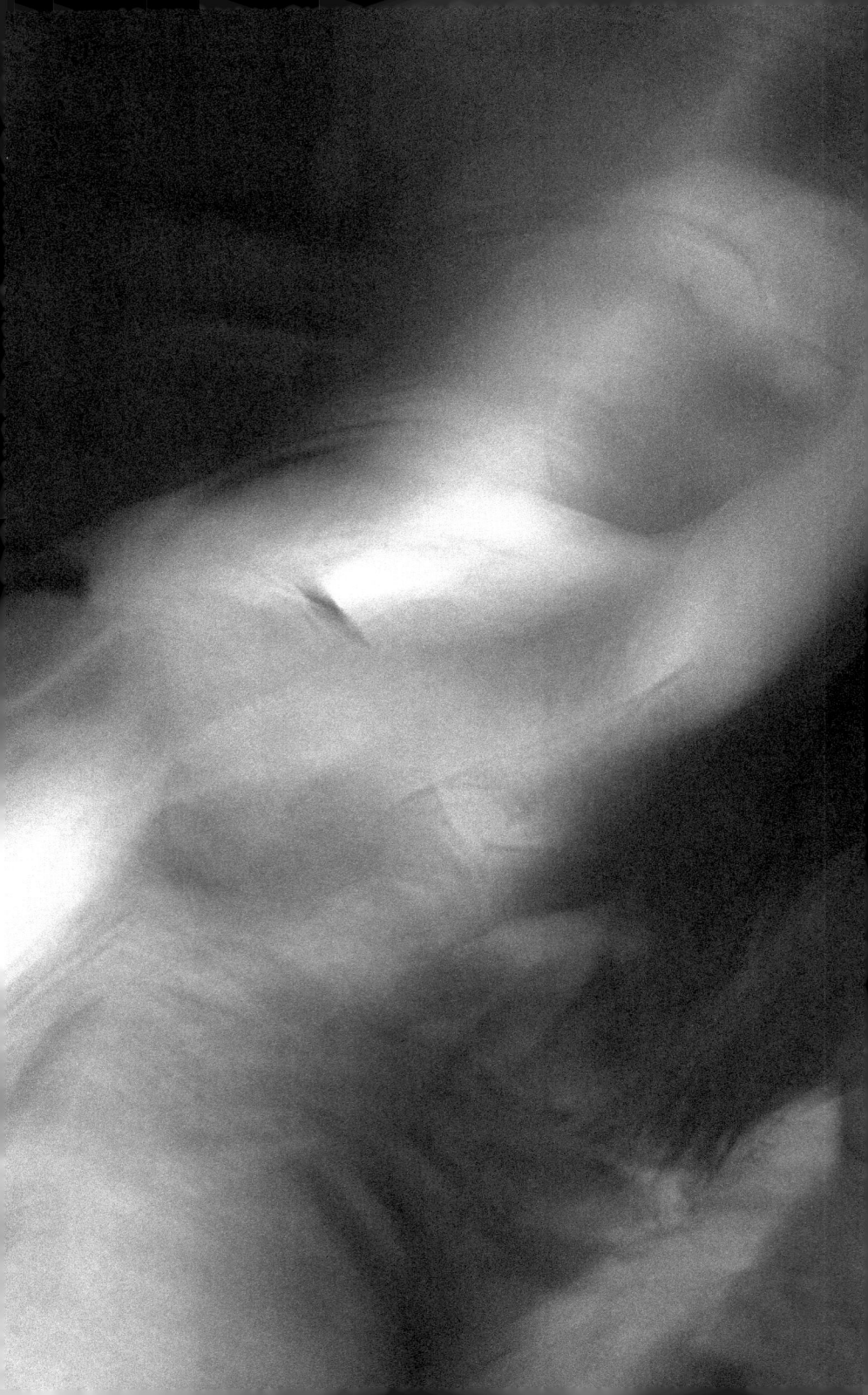

Love Defies Boundaries

Love cares not
For acronyms,
Or labels that define
And constrain,
It does not discriminate
Or pick and choose,
To suit the righteous

When souls collide
In ecstasy and union,
The Universe celebrates,
Regardless of petty strictures
And the dictates of man,
For what is life
Without unconditional love?

Altar of Love

I could spend

    My whole life

        Worshipping

            At the altar

                Of you

Be the Sacred Flame

Be the flame,
Joyfully dancing brightly
Alive to every breath
And change of wind,
In radiant delight
Illuminating the way
With joyous fervour,
Not the candle,
Doomed to sputter
To its foretold ending,
Steadfast bedrock
But never tasting
The gentle caress,
Nay whisper,
Of a Provençal breeze
To set it eagerly alive

Love Does Not Discriminate

Black
      White
            Pink
                  Blue

Gender doesn't matter too

    Love knows no boundaries

        Why should you?

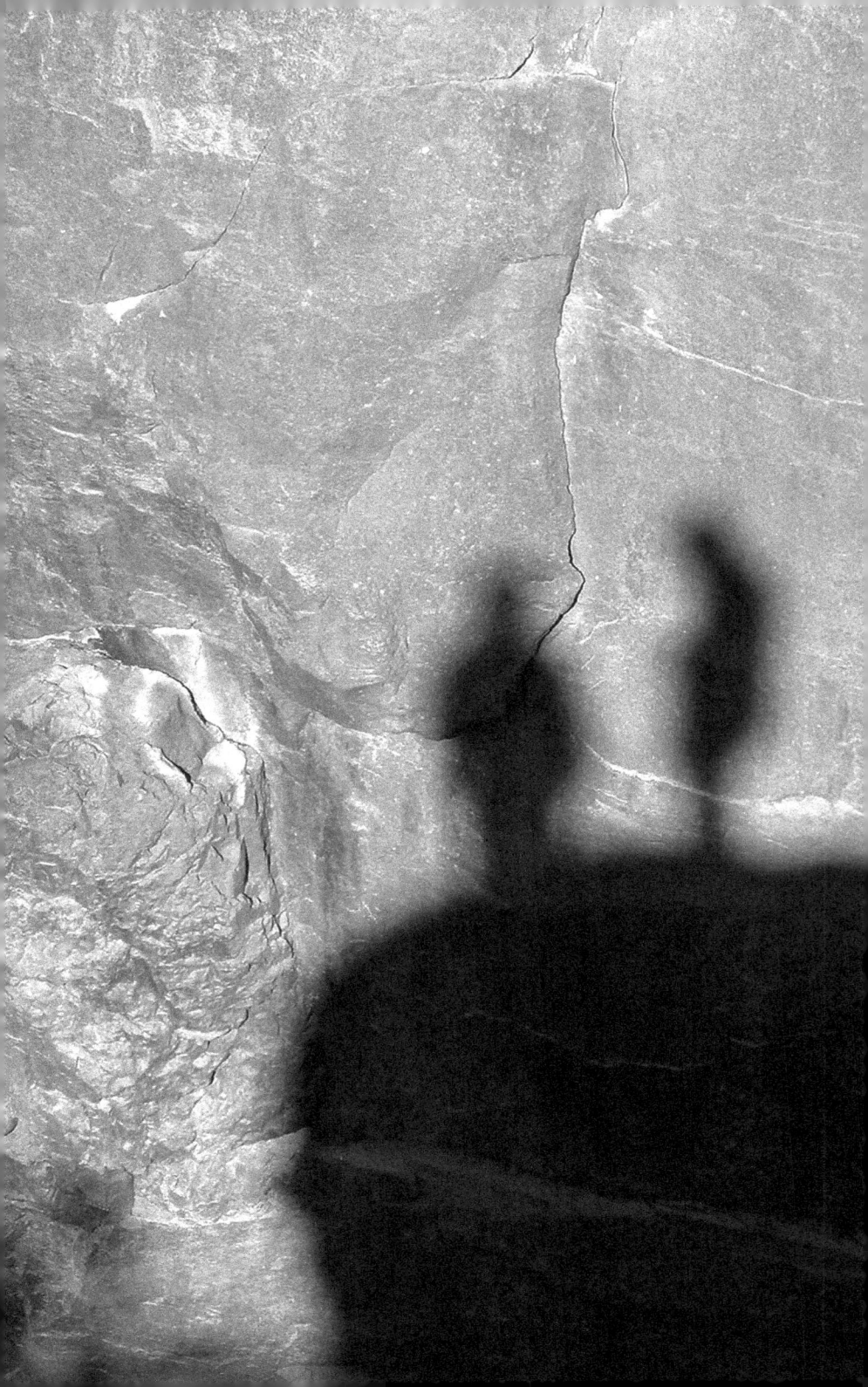

Being Human

We are all damaged
By our experiences,
By choice or happenstance
Both good and bad
Either welcome
Or a feared

But in the end,
It is the distillation,
The captured essences
Of the lives we have lived
That makes us human,
Unique
And worthy.

The Eyes of Love

I could drink

Every day

From your dark

Uncertain eyes

And count myself

Replete in life

And love

Destiny

Do not dwell

On the unattainable

Some things

Are not in your destiny

Embrace All Things

Listen –
    Openly

Speak –
    Truthfully

Love –
    Completely

Who could want more?

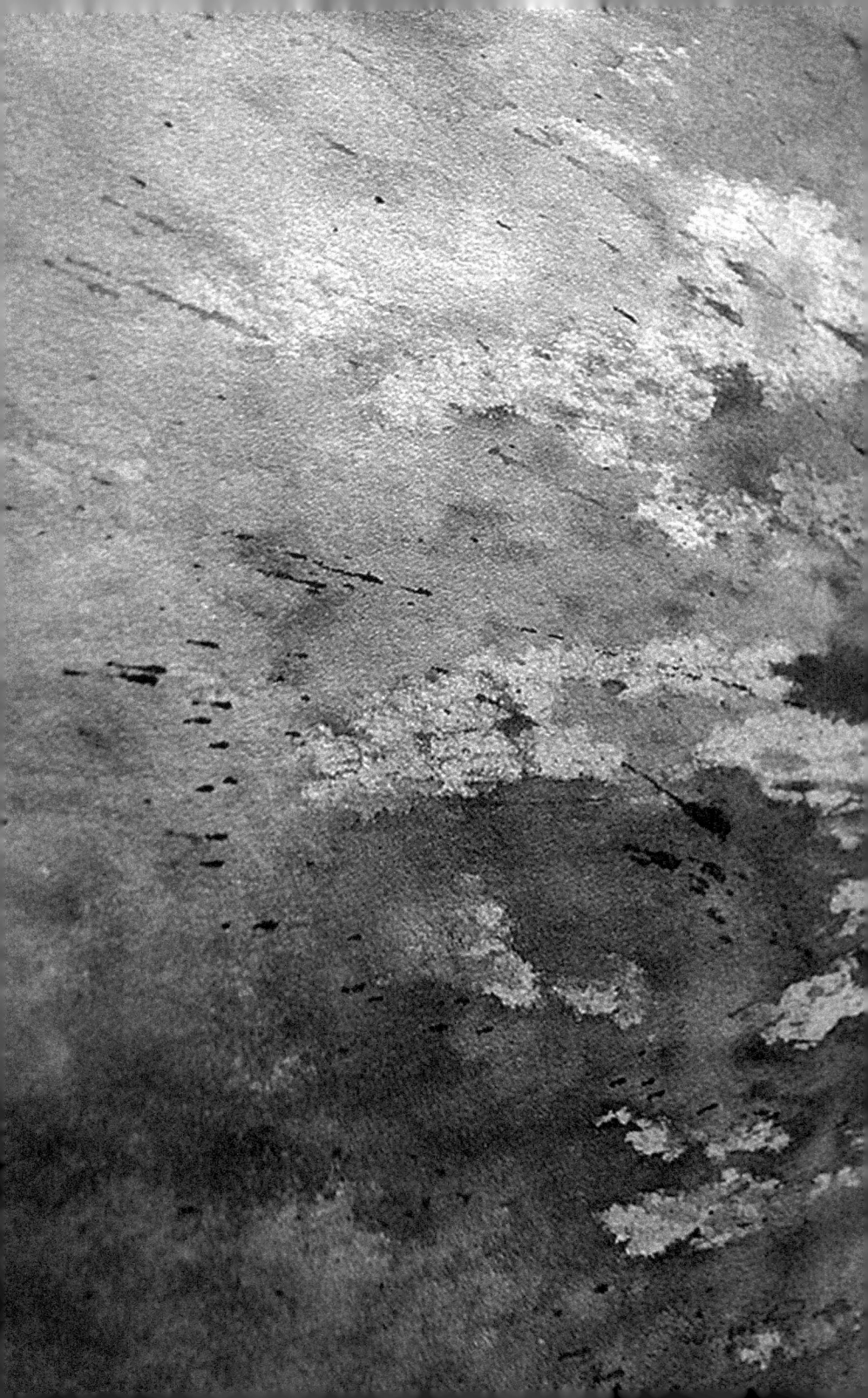

Celestial Union

The attraction between

My molecules and yours

Is biology

The attraction between

My soul and yours

Is love

Lost in Love

The unguarded light

From your eyes

Struck my soul

And extinguished me

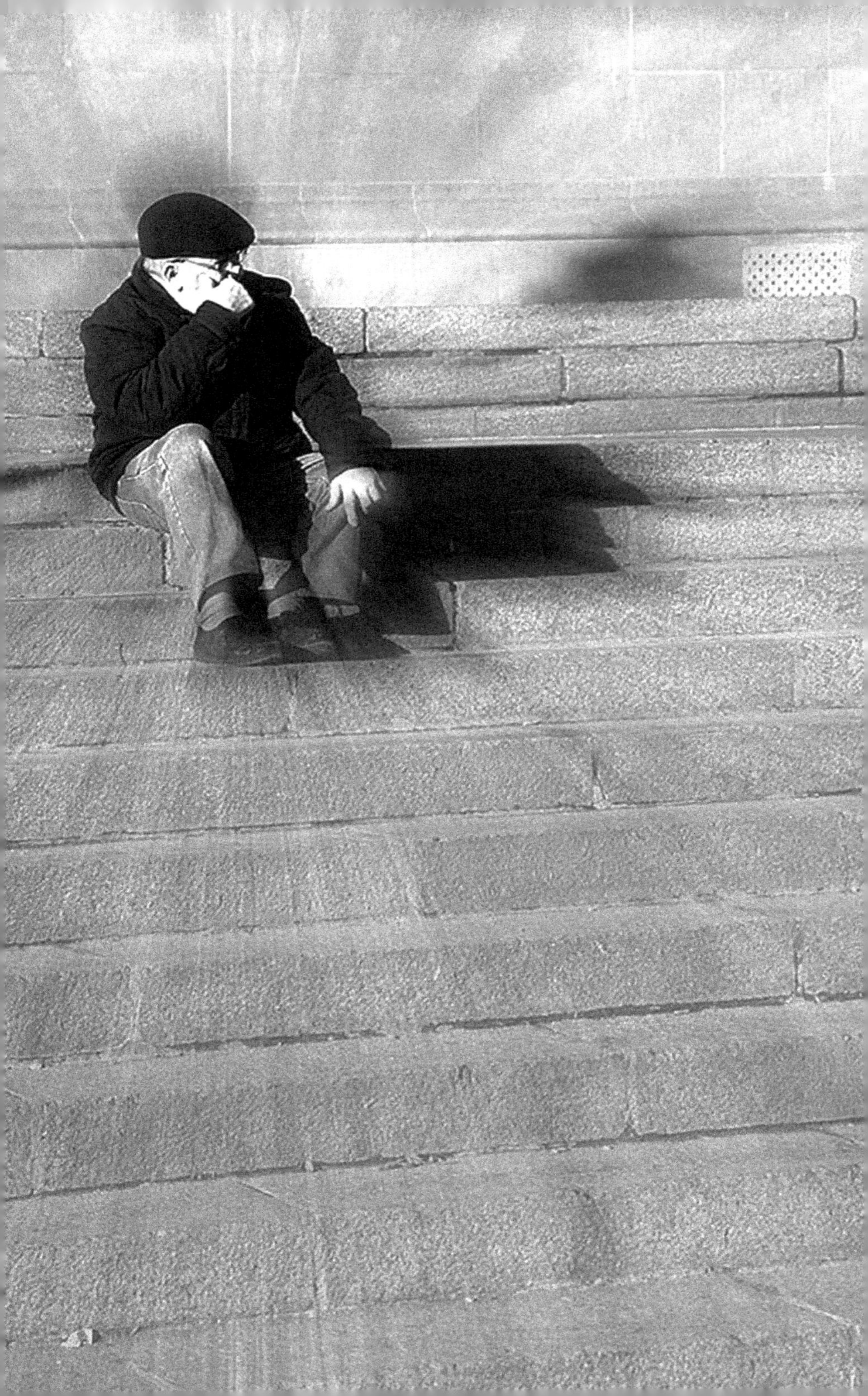

Your Life – Live It

You cannot live

Any life

Other

Than your own

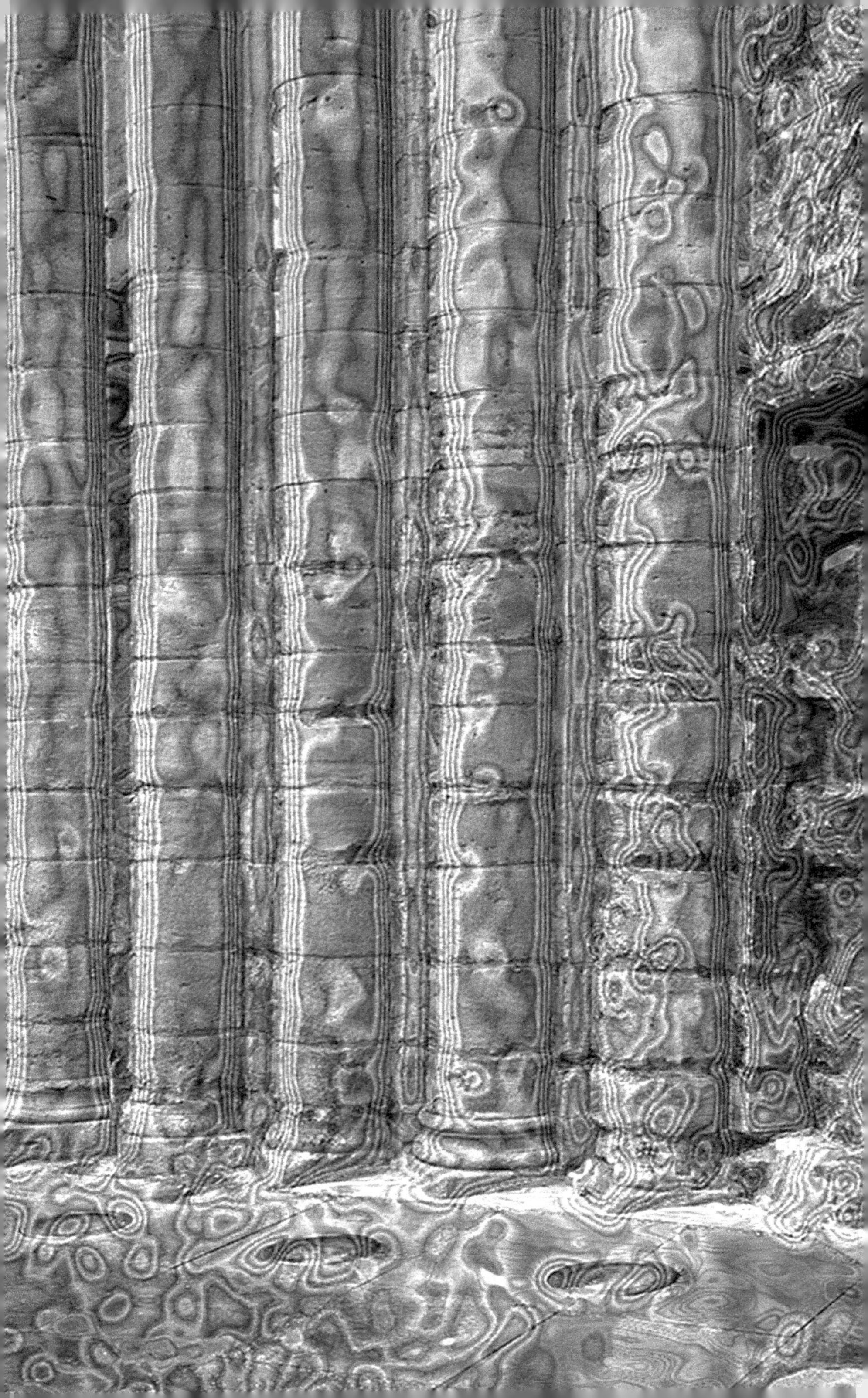

Unconquerable Love

    Love

    Can build empires

    Lay waste civilisations

    Or calm

    The raging sea

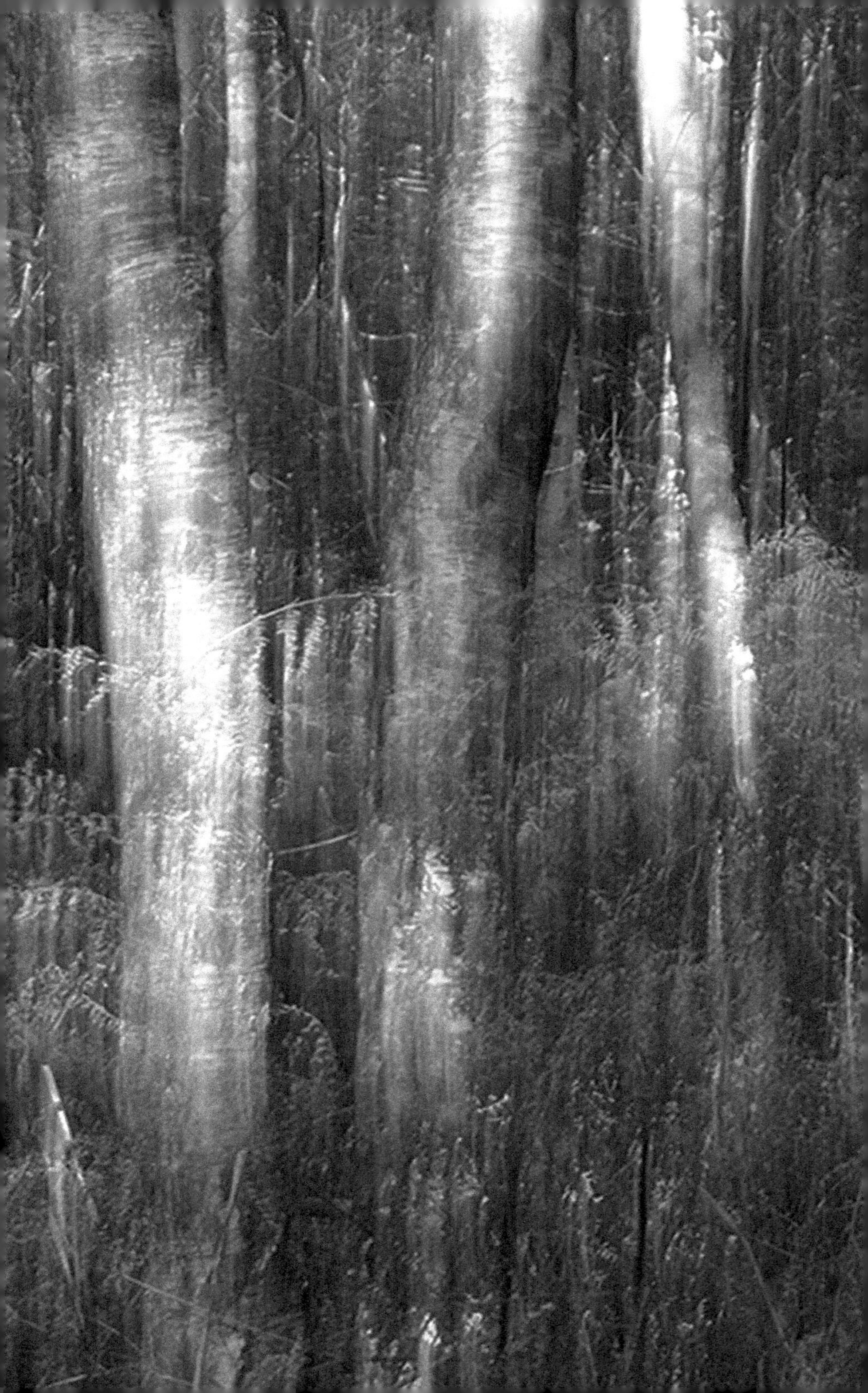

You Cannot Hide from Love

Do not look for love

It will find you

Ready or not!

Keys

Kindness

Opens doors

Smiles

Open hearts

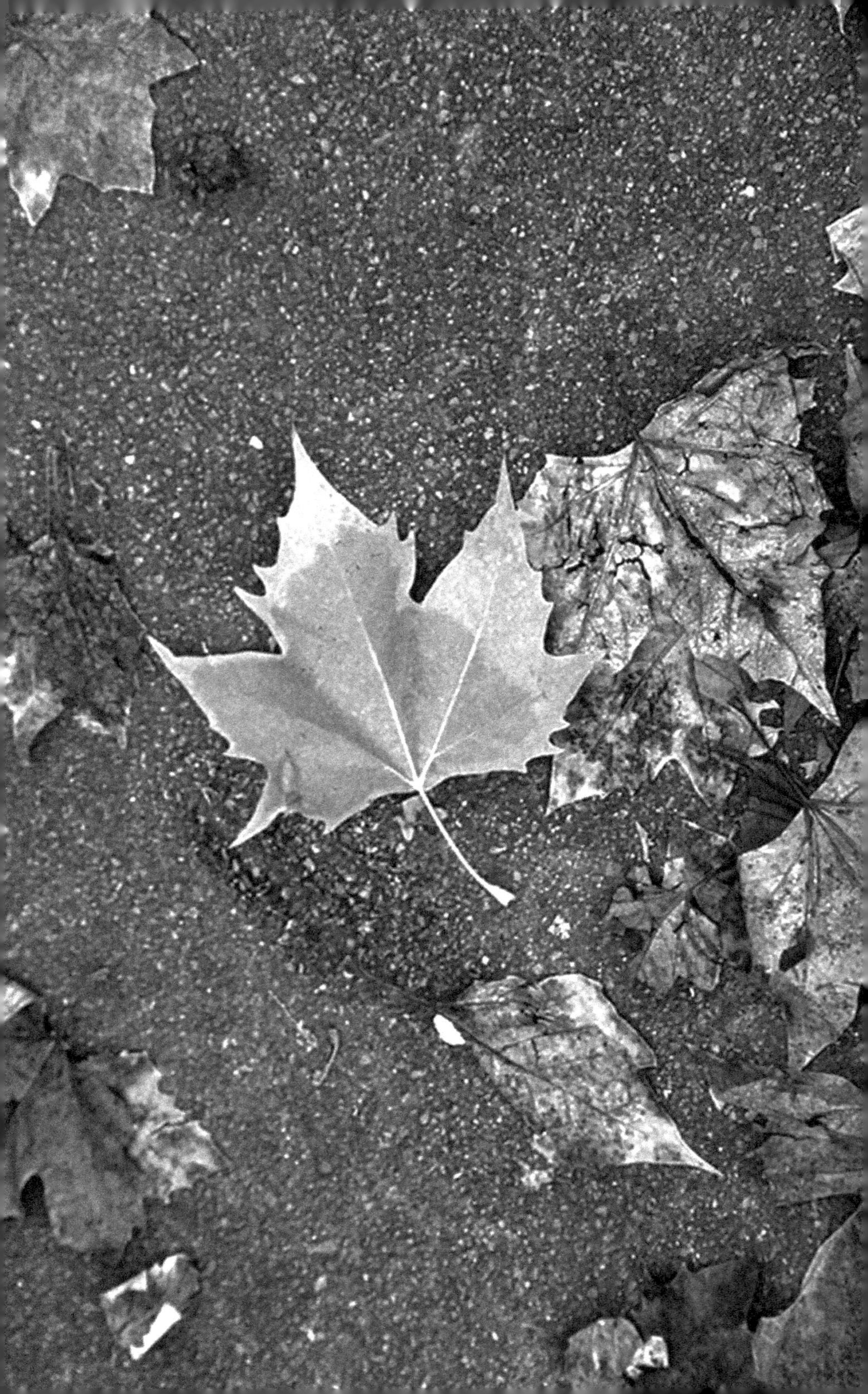

Blessed Rain

Dance in the gentle rain

Unfettered and free

With open heart

And feel the tears

Of your soul

Fall softly away

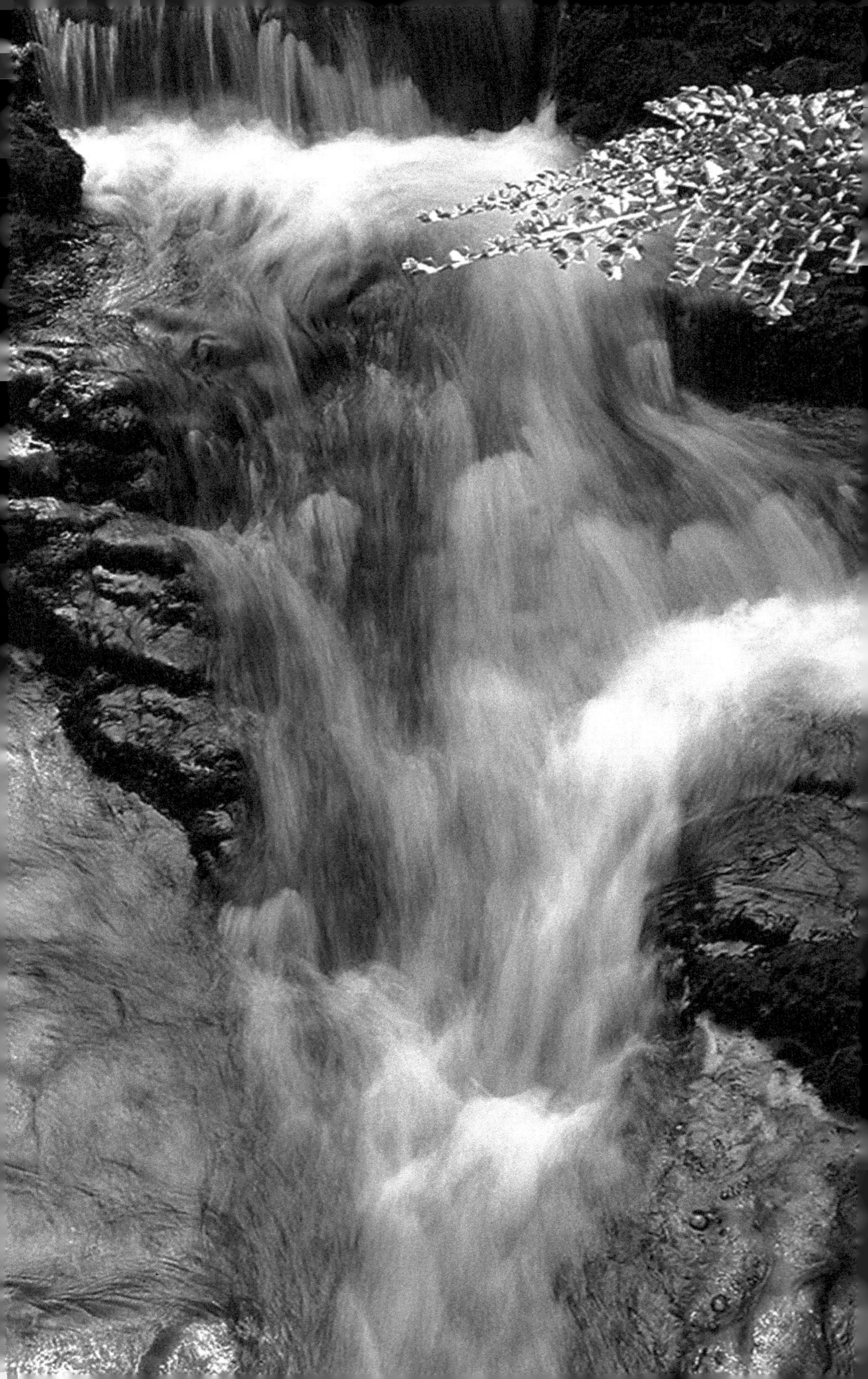

Life is the Journey

The sound

And the silence

Pass through

The door of understanding

To tread hesitantly

The pathless journey

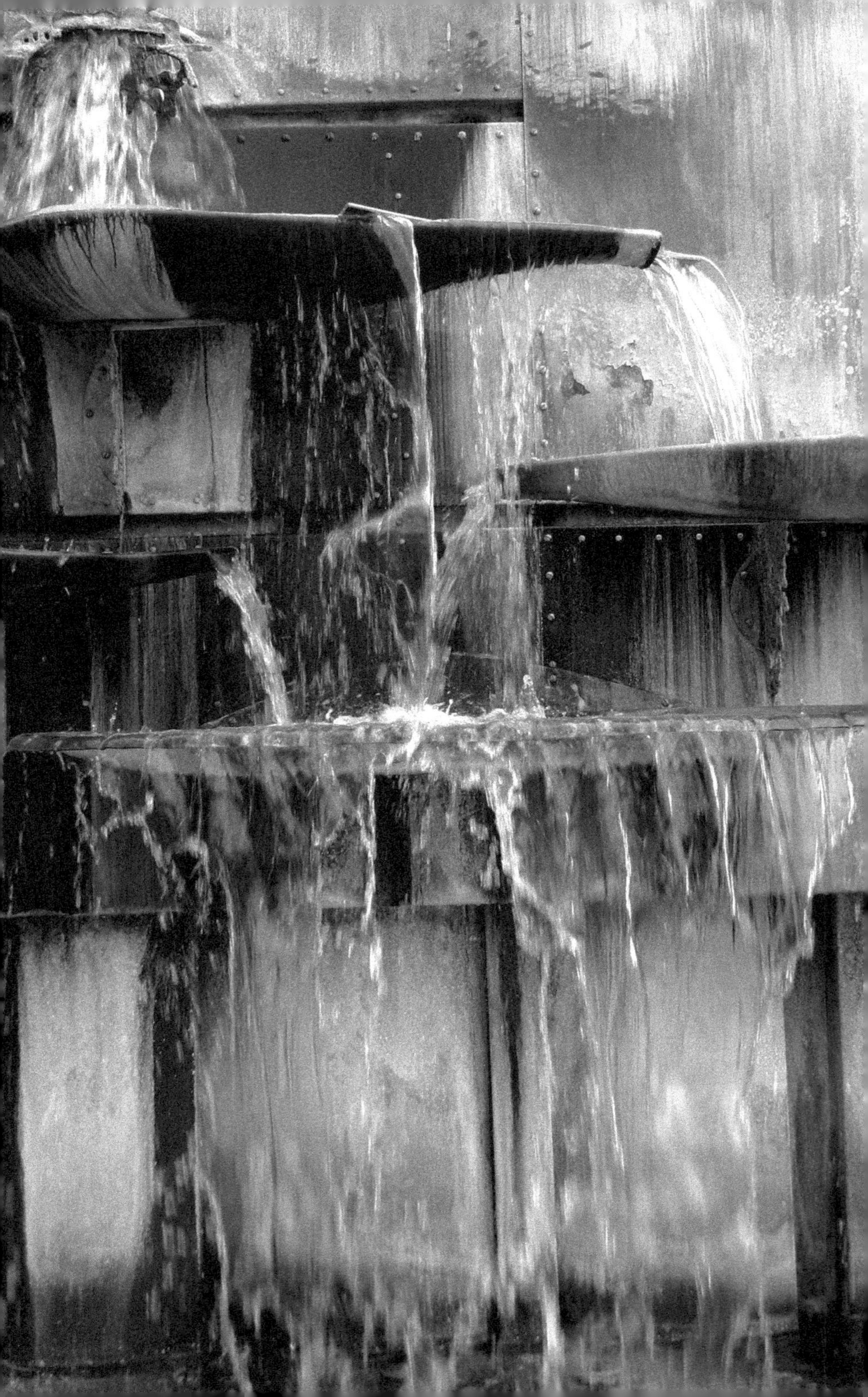

Pure Heart

If your heart is pure

There is nothing

That you need

Be ashamed of

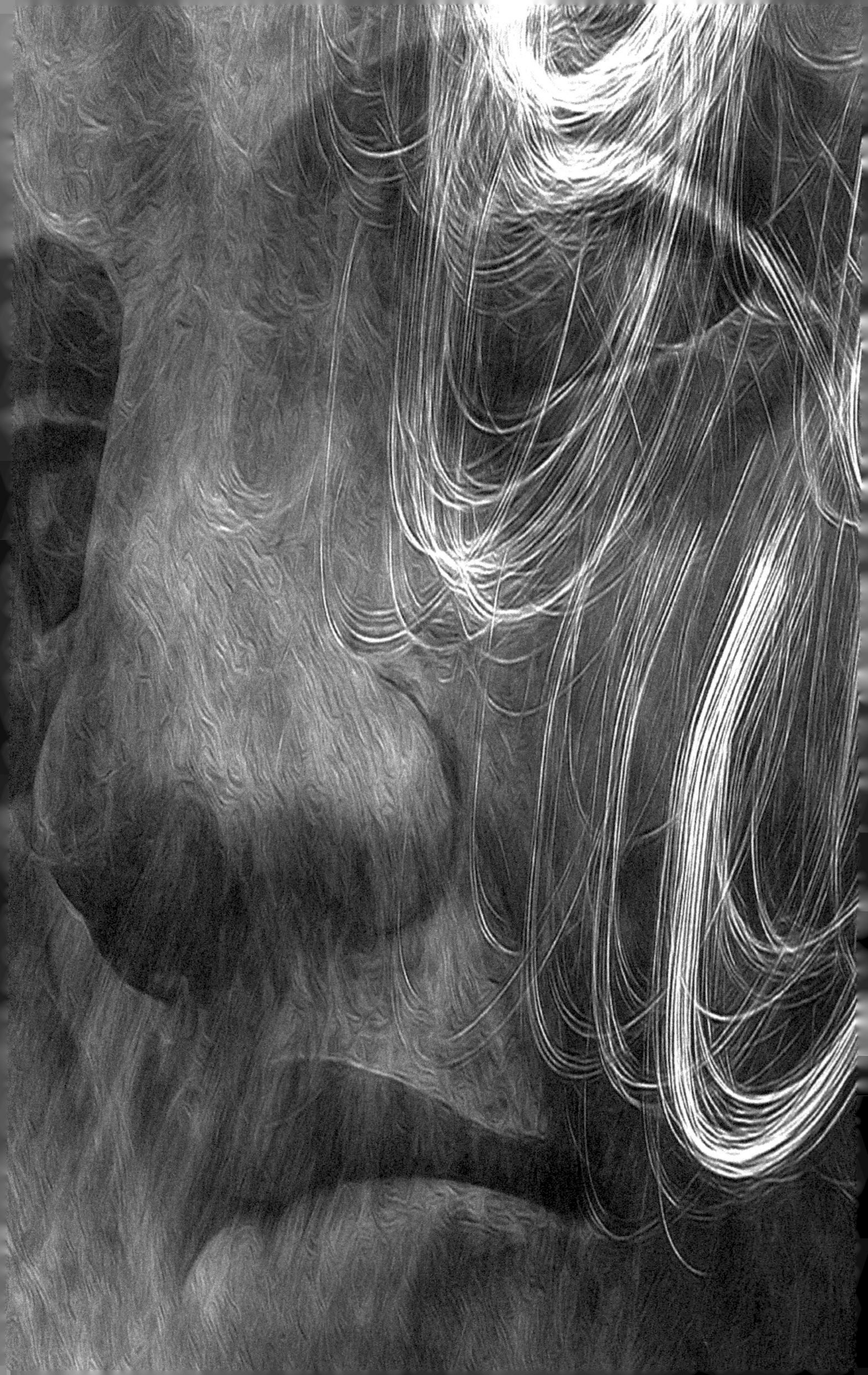

Fatal Attraction

One open glance

Your hesitant smile

Were enough

To doom me

To a life

Of longing

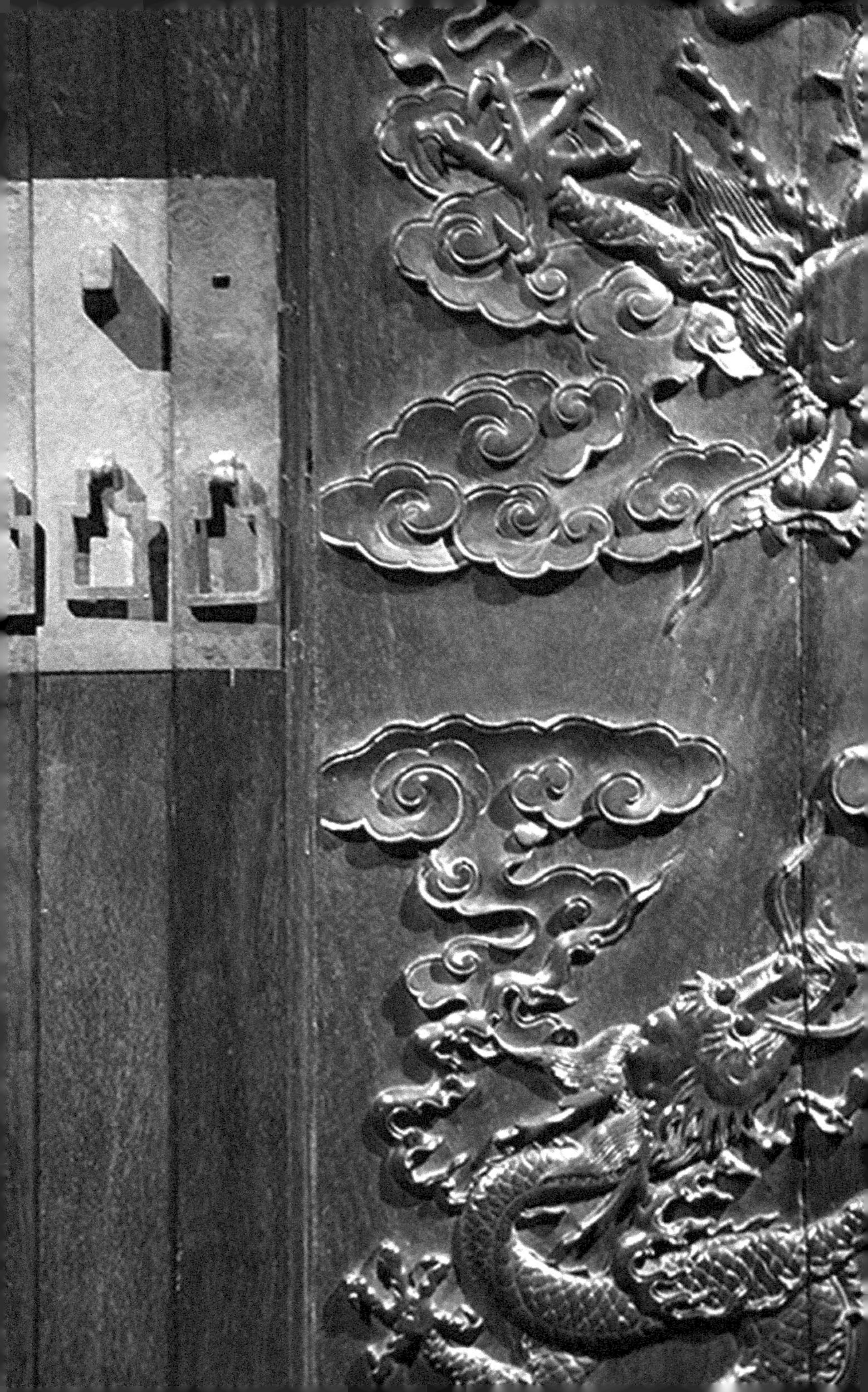

Feel My Breath

Feel my breath
Caress your beloved face
In the gentle passing
Of a whispered breeze

Feel my yearning
In your aching heart
And the haunting cry
Of the eagle in flight

And feel my love
Enfold you softly
In the darkest night
And the crystal dawn

For you are my life
My one great love
My every desire
And my ever after

Foundations of Love

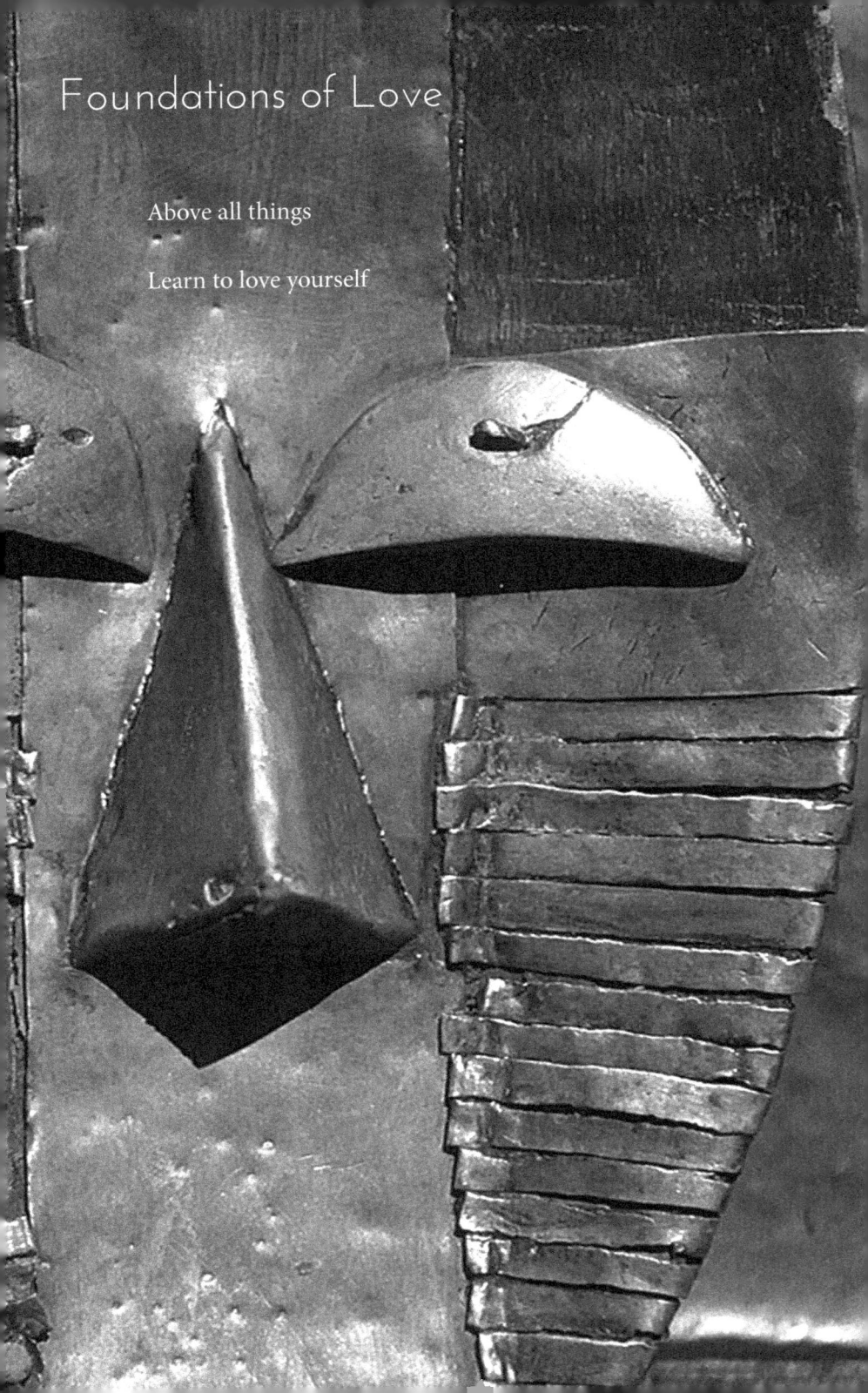

Above all things

Learn to love yourself

BECOME

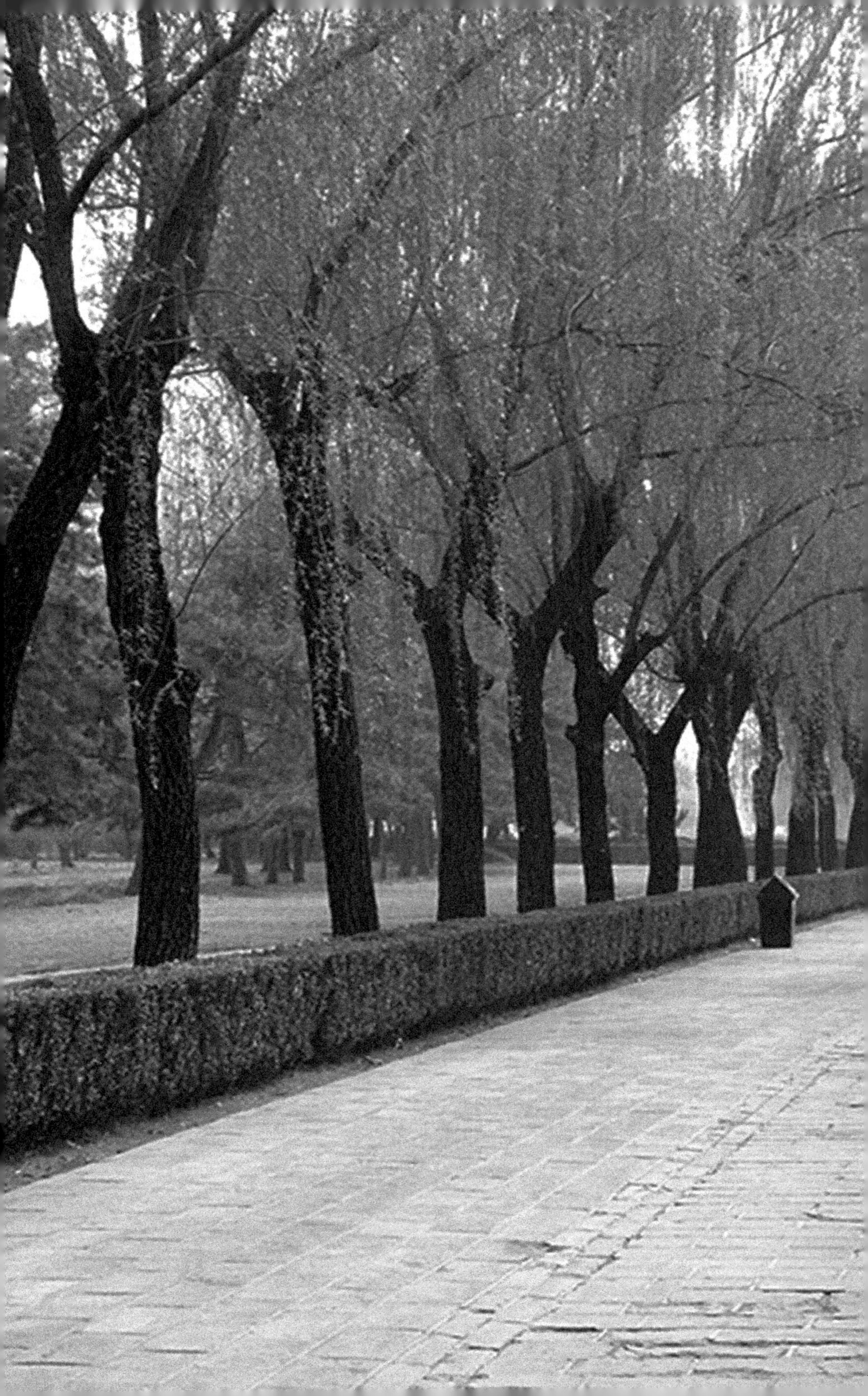

The Journey

We set out

On this journey

Of us unfolding

In search of truth

And joy

To find that life

May have other plans

Or paths in mind

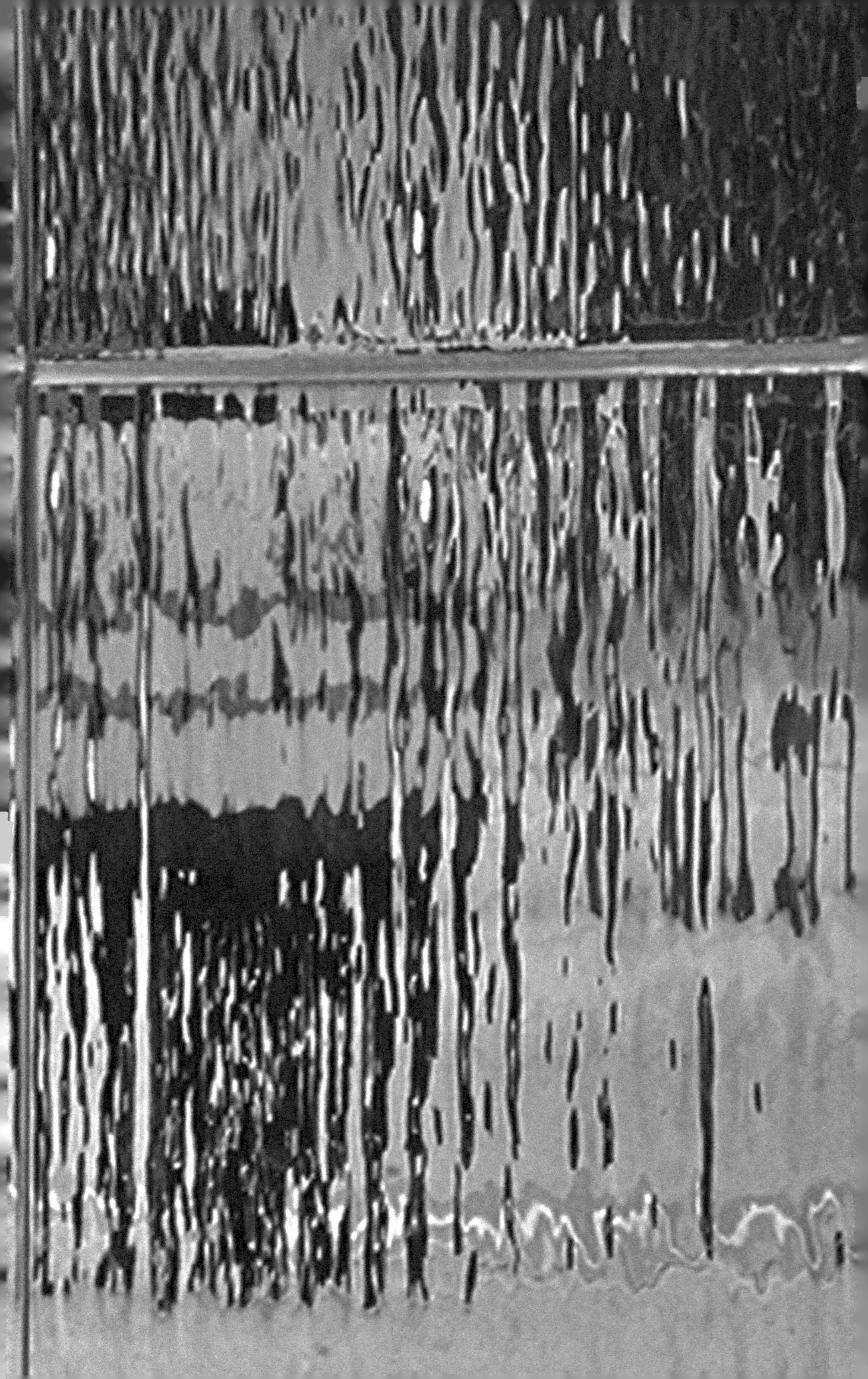

It was Always There

We tore each other apart

Looking for unconditional love

You and I

Only to find

That it was there

All along

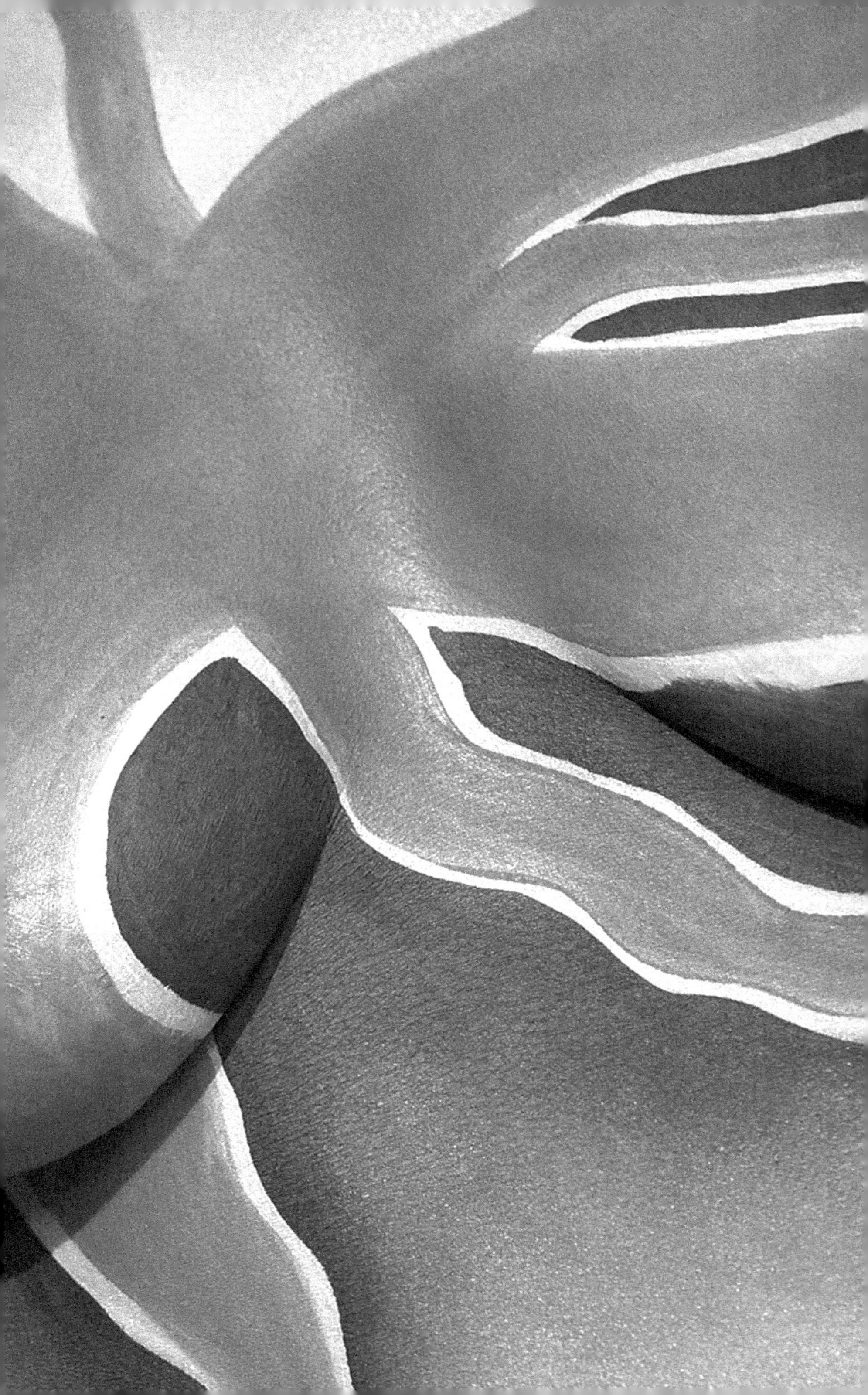

Dedication

Without conscious thought

Or grand design

We gave so much

Of ourselves to the world

That there was nothing left

For us to draw from

When hope died

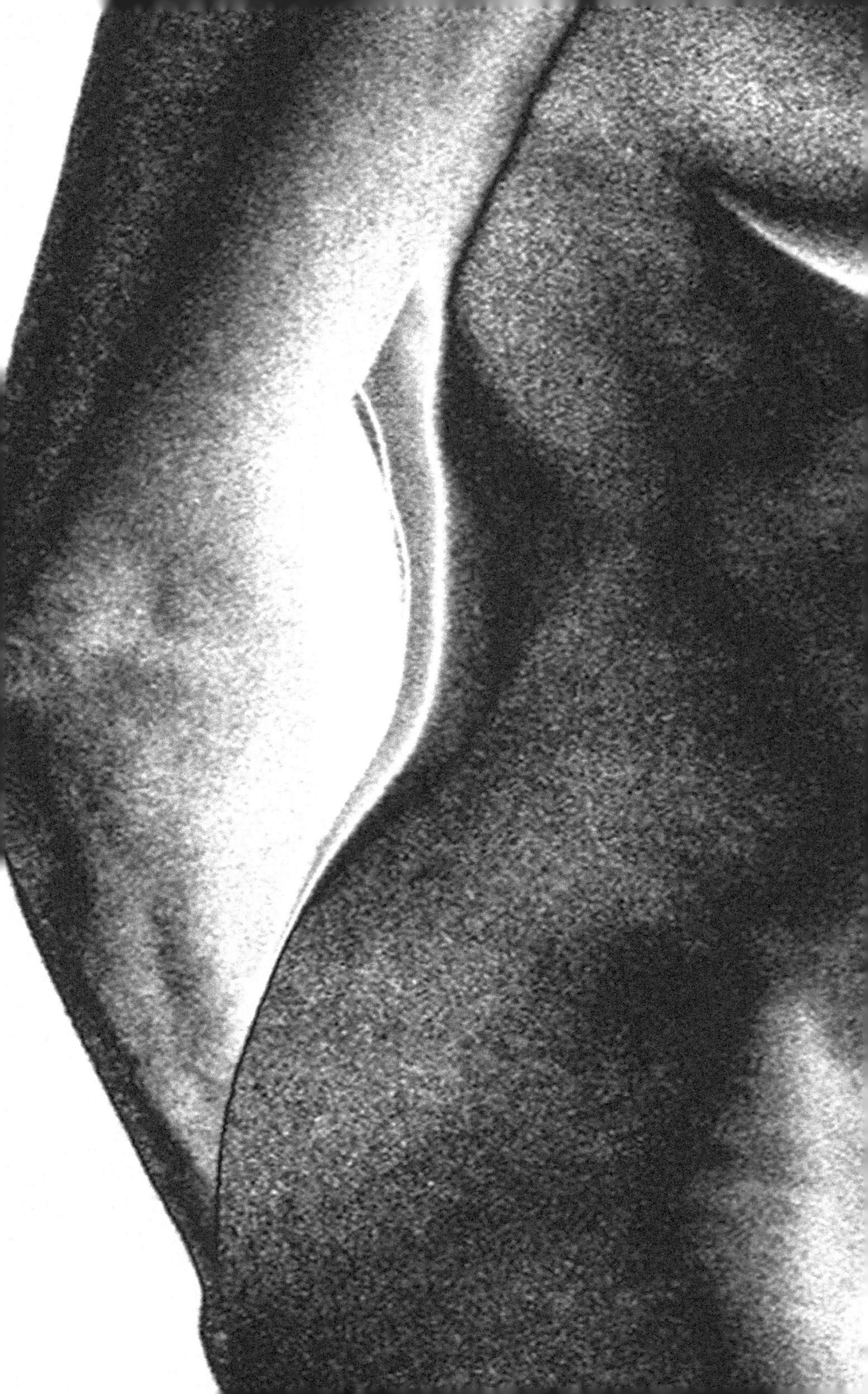

Undressed

Undressed you are a different being
Far from couture
And social niceties
Which fall effortlessly
From your eager body
In myriad rooms of dark intent
A more primal creature
Thus revealed and released
To momentary abandon and delight
That feeds a deeper craving
For this instant, at least

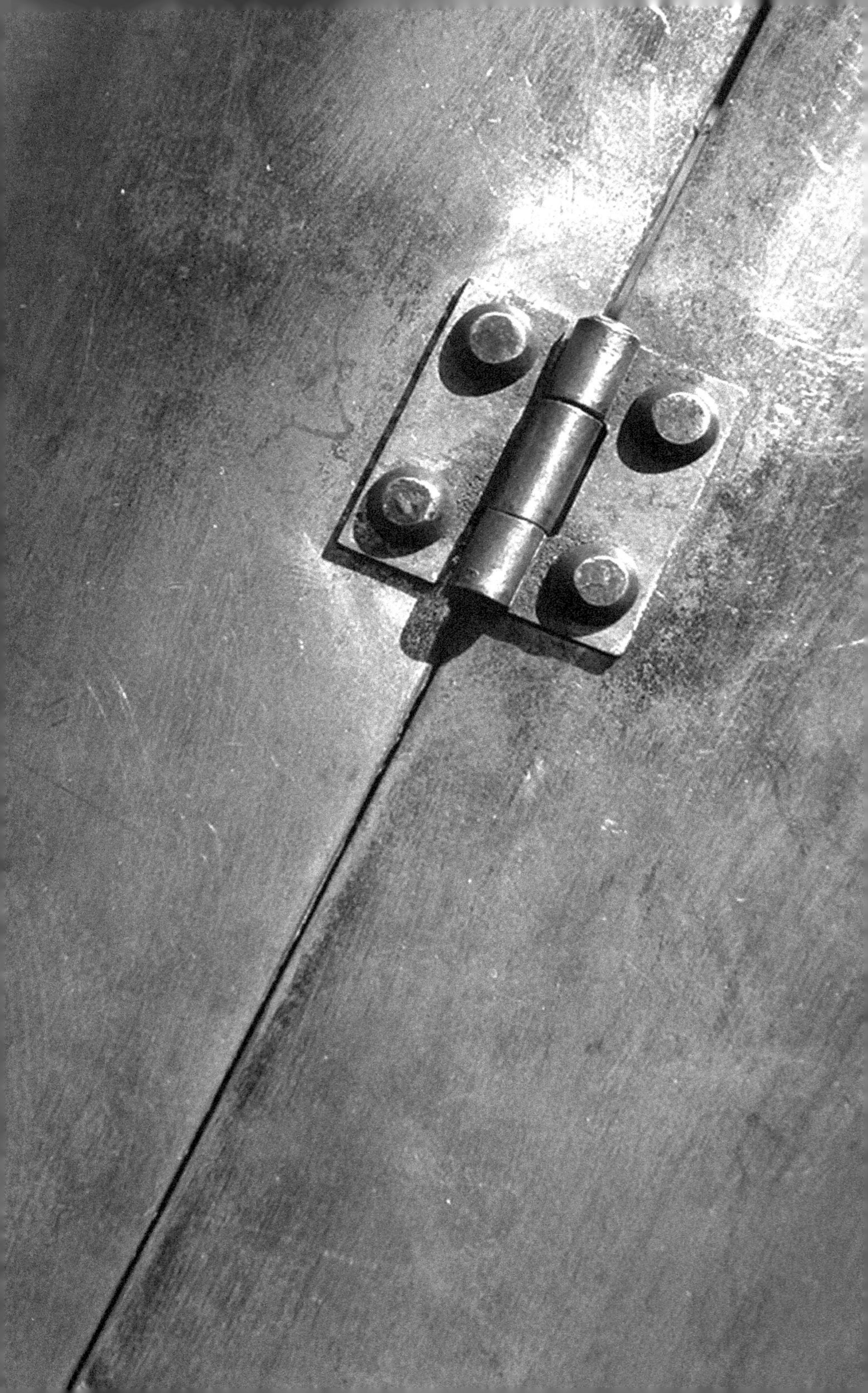

Illusions of Love

In furtive rooms

Of desperate intent

And frantic coupling

You grasp with unquenchable hunger

For even the momentary

Illusion of love

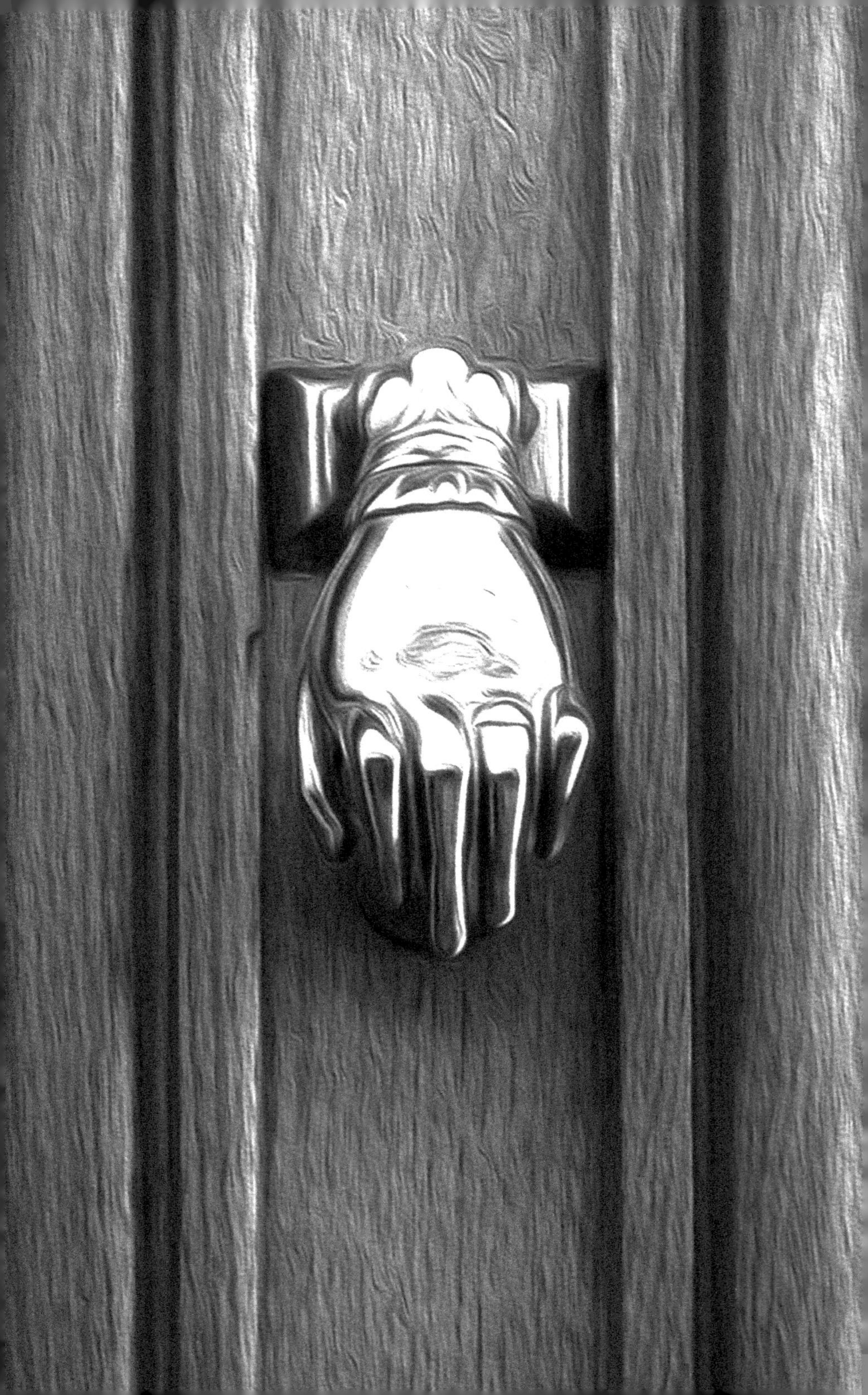

Creation

Sex is sacred

It is creation laid bare

Taking us back

To the beginning

Of all things

Transcending animal instinct

And revealing our

Inherent divinity

With each act symbolising

The origins of life

Differences

Enquiring mind
Or tortured soul
The consequences seem
Quite the same

Embers of Love

Yet even in the darkest hour

The embers of hope remain

In the hesitant embrace

Of an open heart

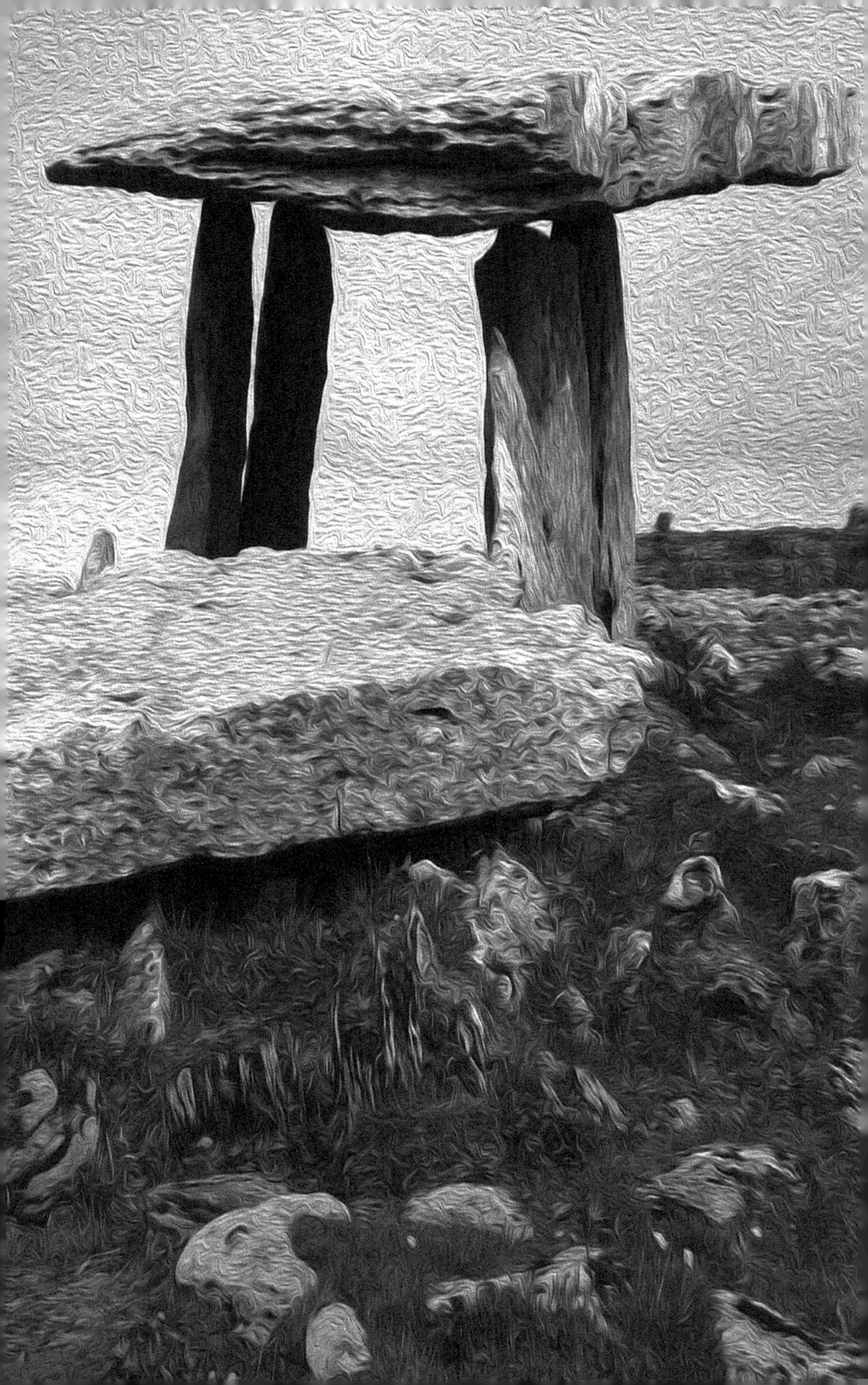

Clinging to the Past

At some point

You have to let it go,

Otherwise, it is not healing,

It is not climbing life's mountain together

In unison and harmony,

You are simply raking through the farmyard,

Looking for more shit to throw!

Gentle Hand

Across the desolate wastelands

Of my parched

And shattered soul

You offered your gentle hand

And loved me whole

Corrosion

Do not confuse
Criticism and contempt
For concern and compassion.
I don't!

Age

Time
And life
Diminish
Us all.

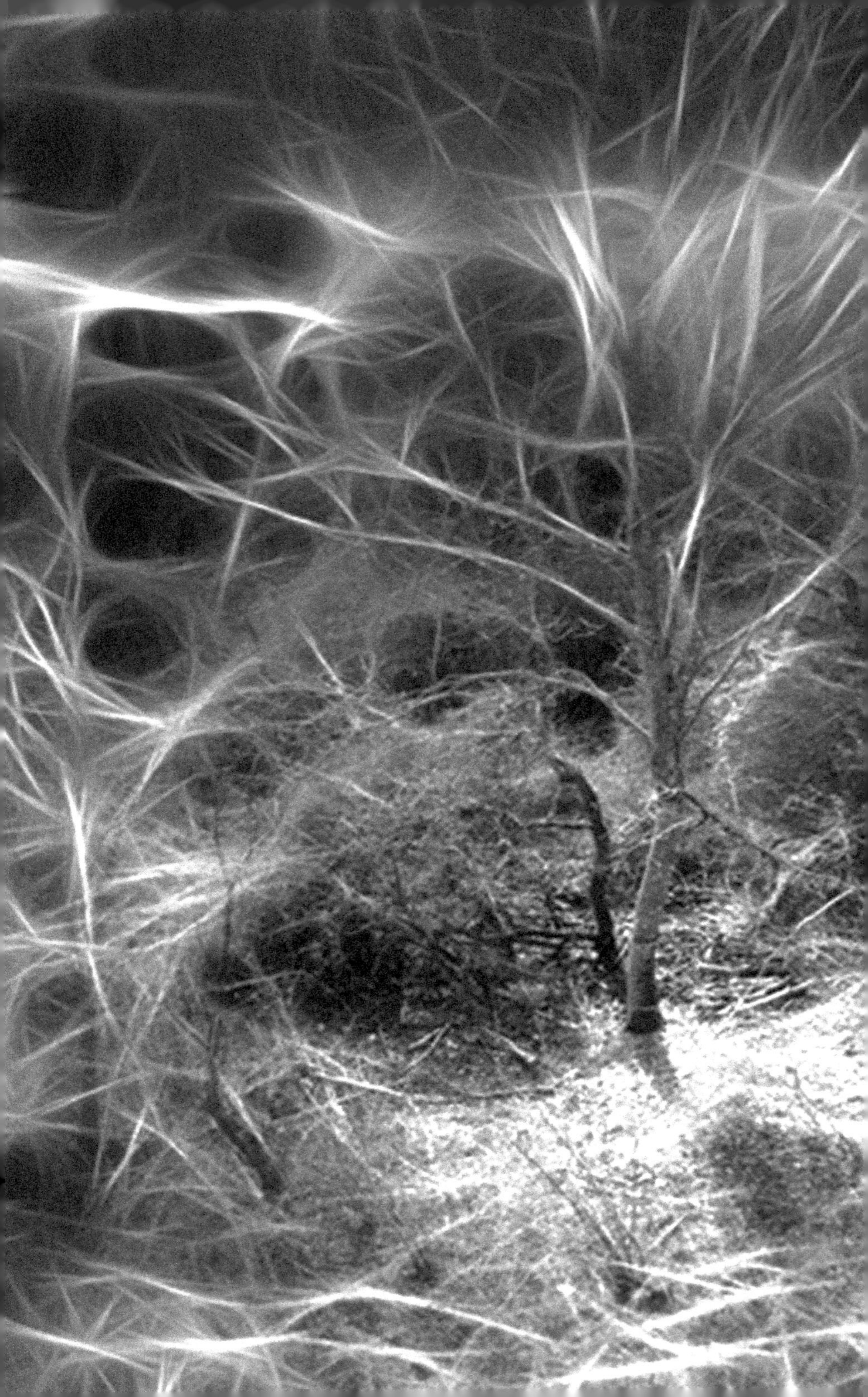

Perspectives

When everything around you

Looks like weeds and desolation

And you don't know

Which way to look or turn

Remember that from the heavens

It all looks like a garden

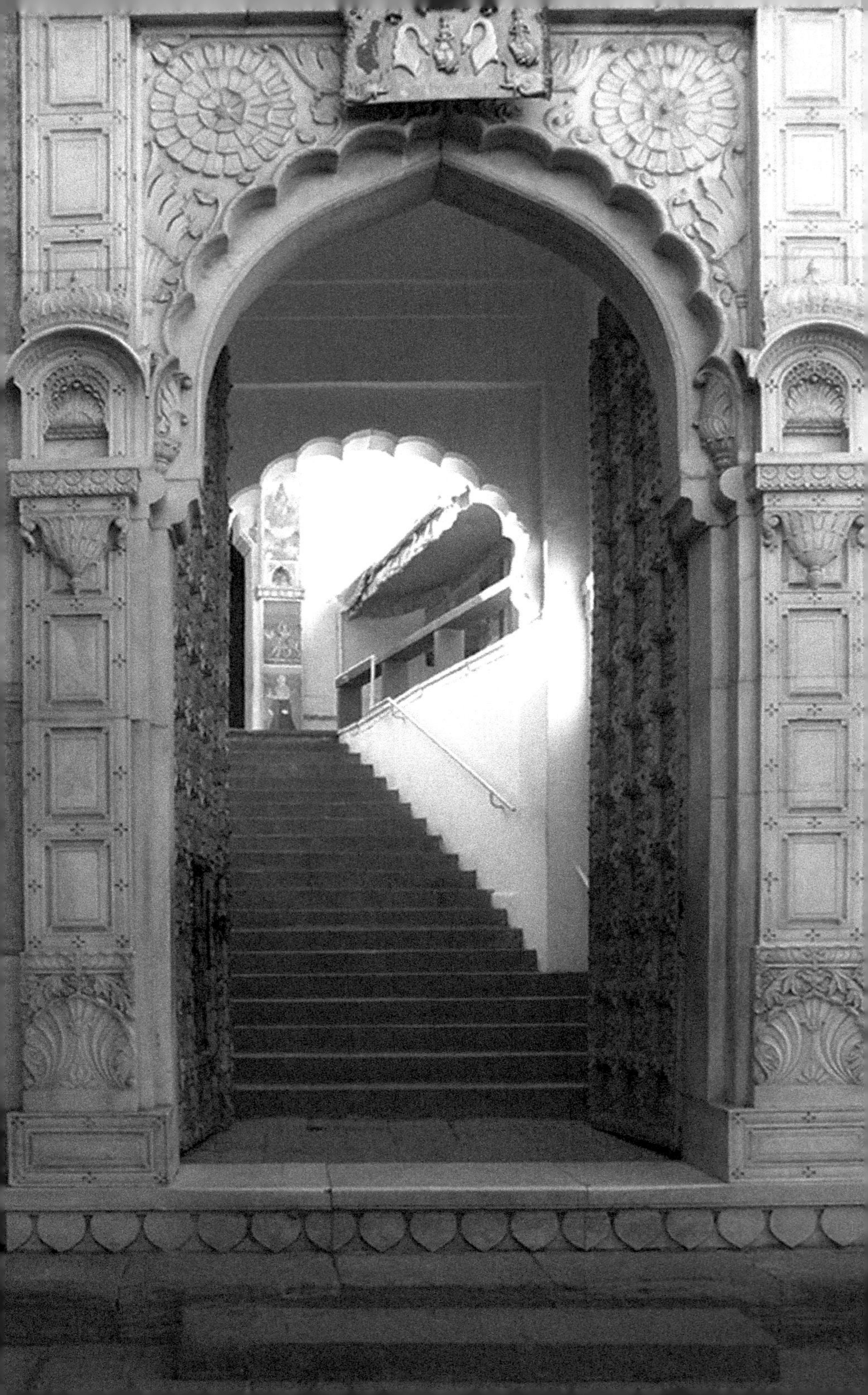

Open Your Mind

The paths of darkness
Are labyrinthine
And without end.
How can they not be?
For in the shifting,
Shapeless mind
Fact and fiction mingle seamlessly
To manufacture their webs,
Their deceits
Which serve only to blind you
To the truth and beauty all around.

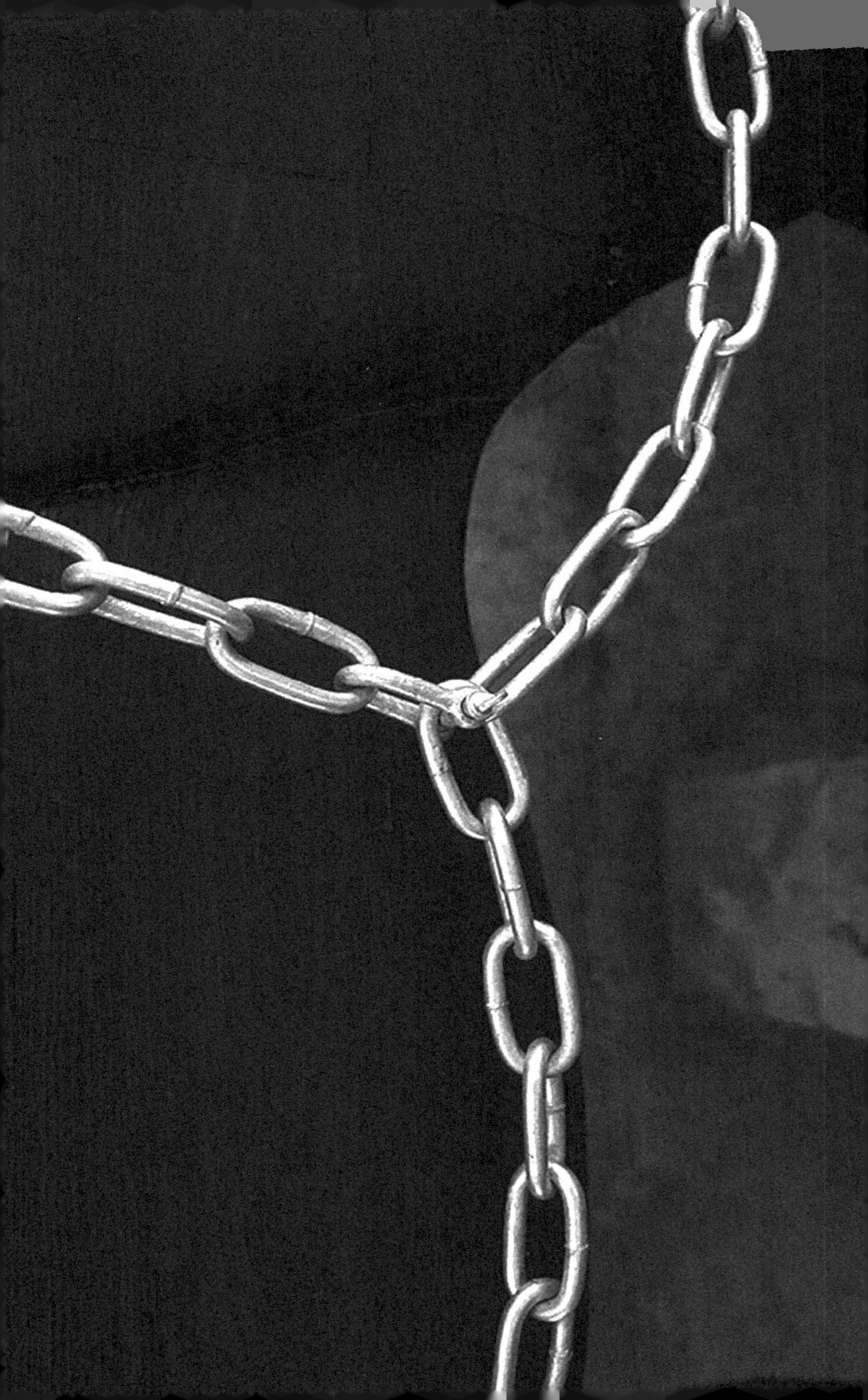

Distrust Destroys

I am not worthy

Of your distrust

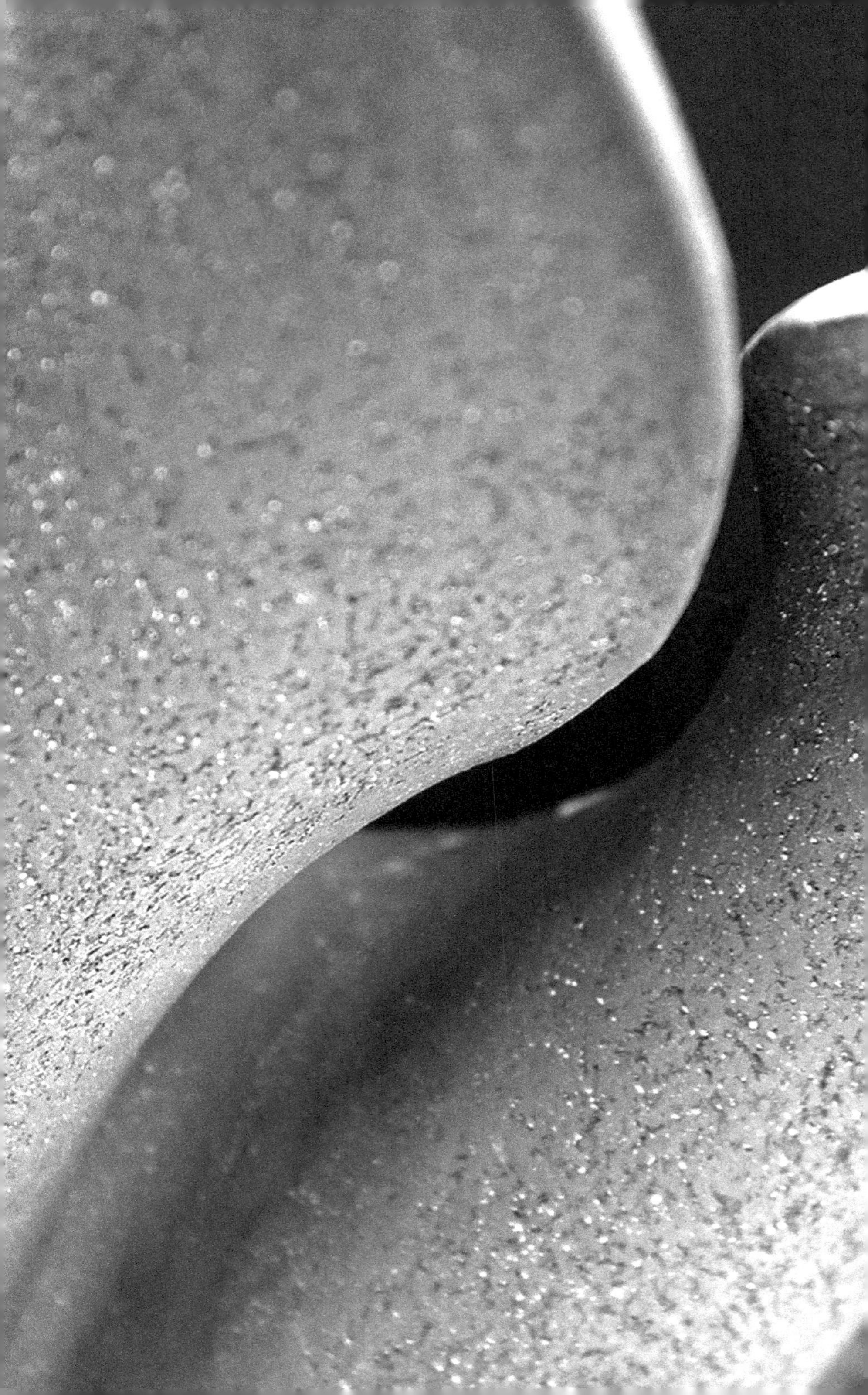

Past Present

We may be moulded

By the past

But that does not

Pre-ordain our future

Courage

Find the courage

To think for yourself

The Past

Let the past go,
Unmolested, un-regretted,
There are challenges enough
In each moment
To occupy you
For all time

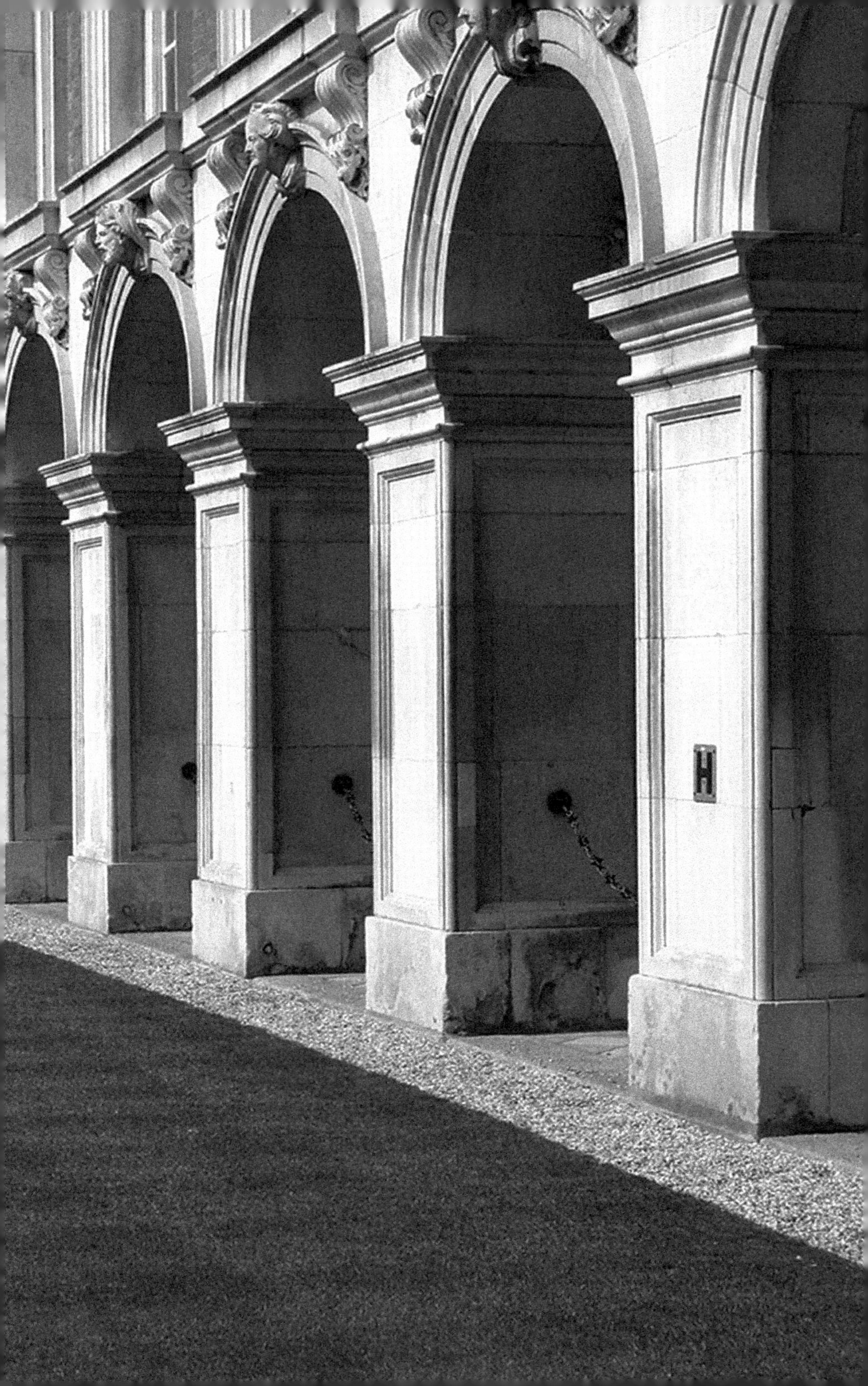
H

Break Down the Walls

So stone
By painful stone
You build the pillars
And colonnades
Of your past self

Filling the corridors
With uncertain memories
And hesitant desire

Whilst all the while
The sun shines bright
And wholesome
Outside the walls.

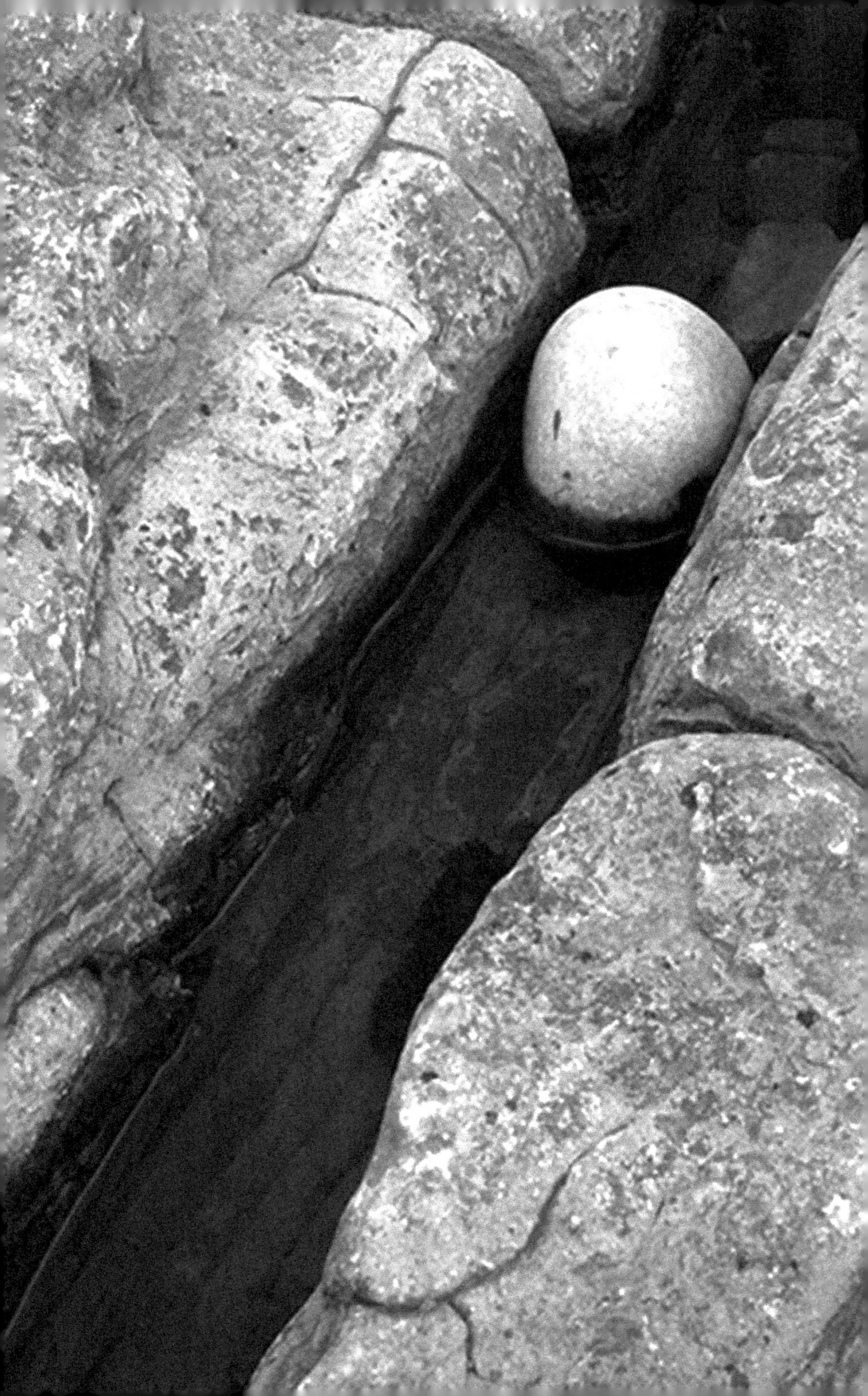

Take the Path

Paths cannot be taught

They can only be taken

P. TENER

DI CARRA

MDCCC

Loving Sex

If sex
Is all that you have
Then you have nothing
Just biology and primal lust

Love gives you freedom
Not chains
Nor regrets

Love is simply a dance
Of two hearts
Straining to beat
As one

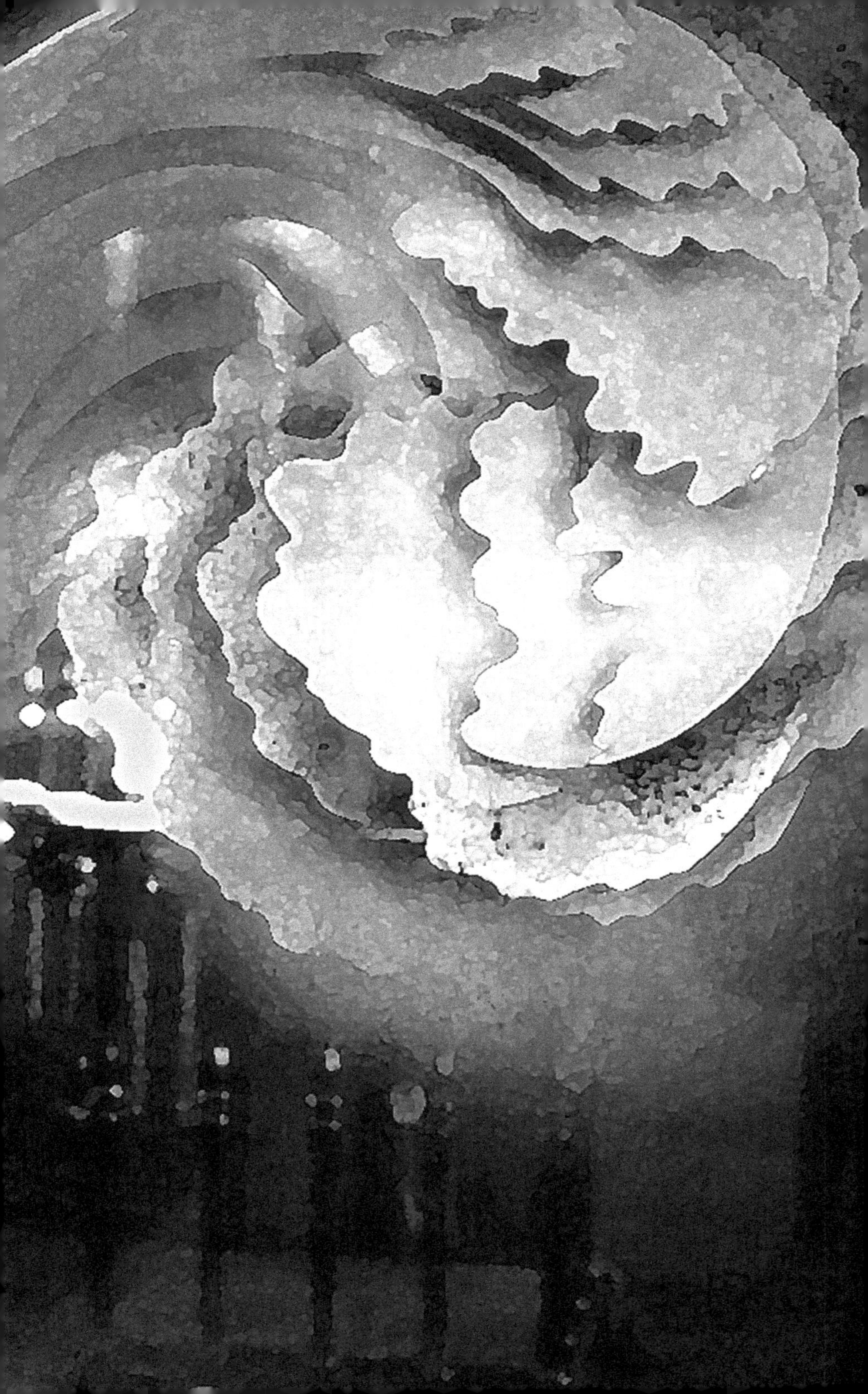

Love Overwhelms Us

When love threatens
To overwhelm you
Drowning in a sea
Of unanchored emotion
And hesitant steps
Of painful recollection
Let yourself go
Into that wondrous unknown
With hope and desire
For there is as much
Living ahead
As there is in the past

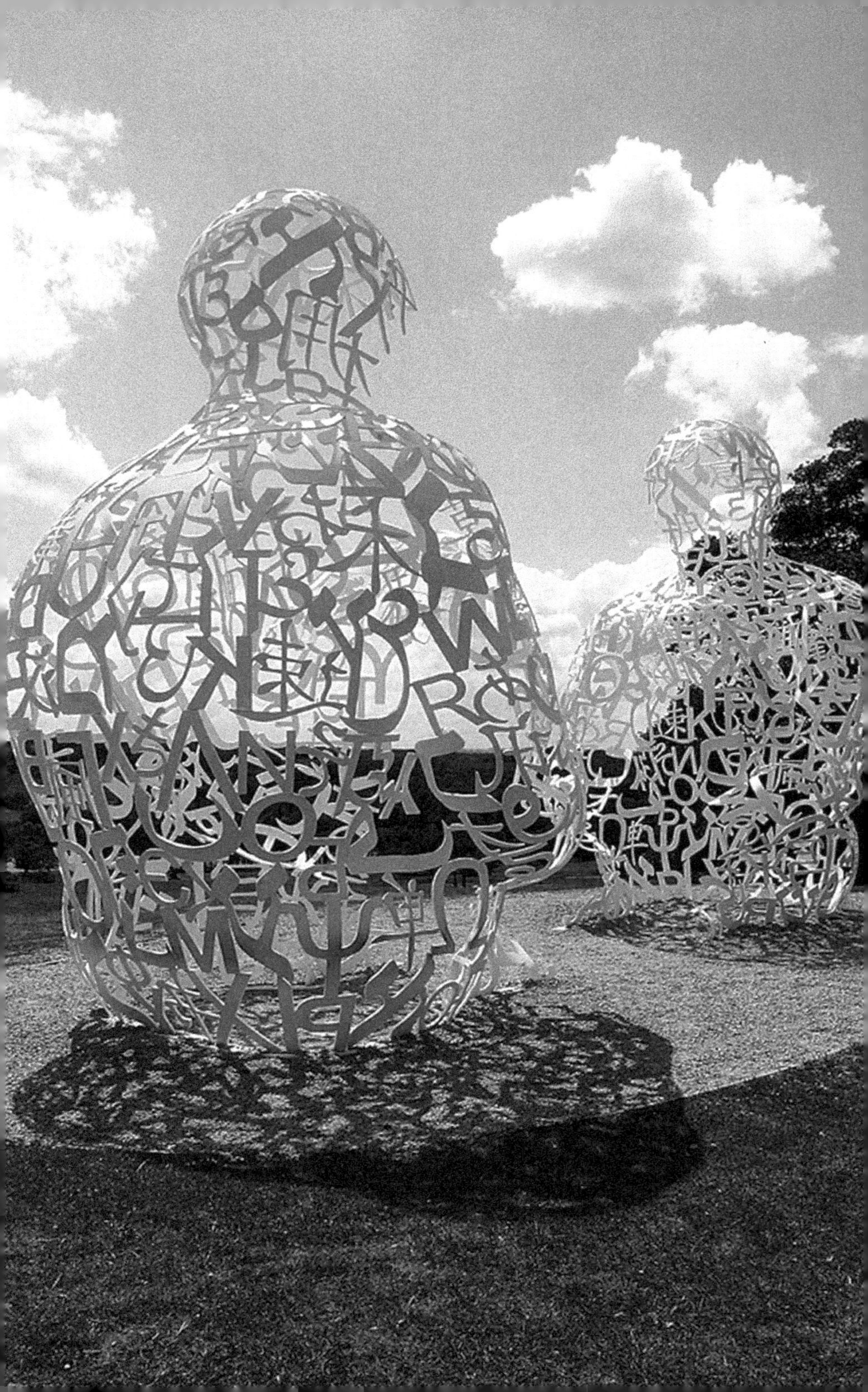

Emotional Scars

What would you look like

If you wore your emotional scars

On the outside?

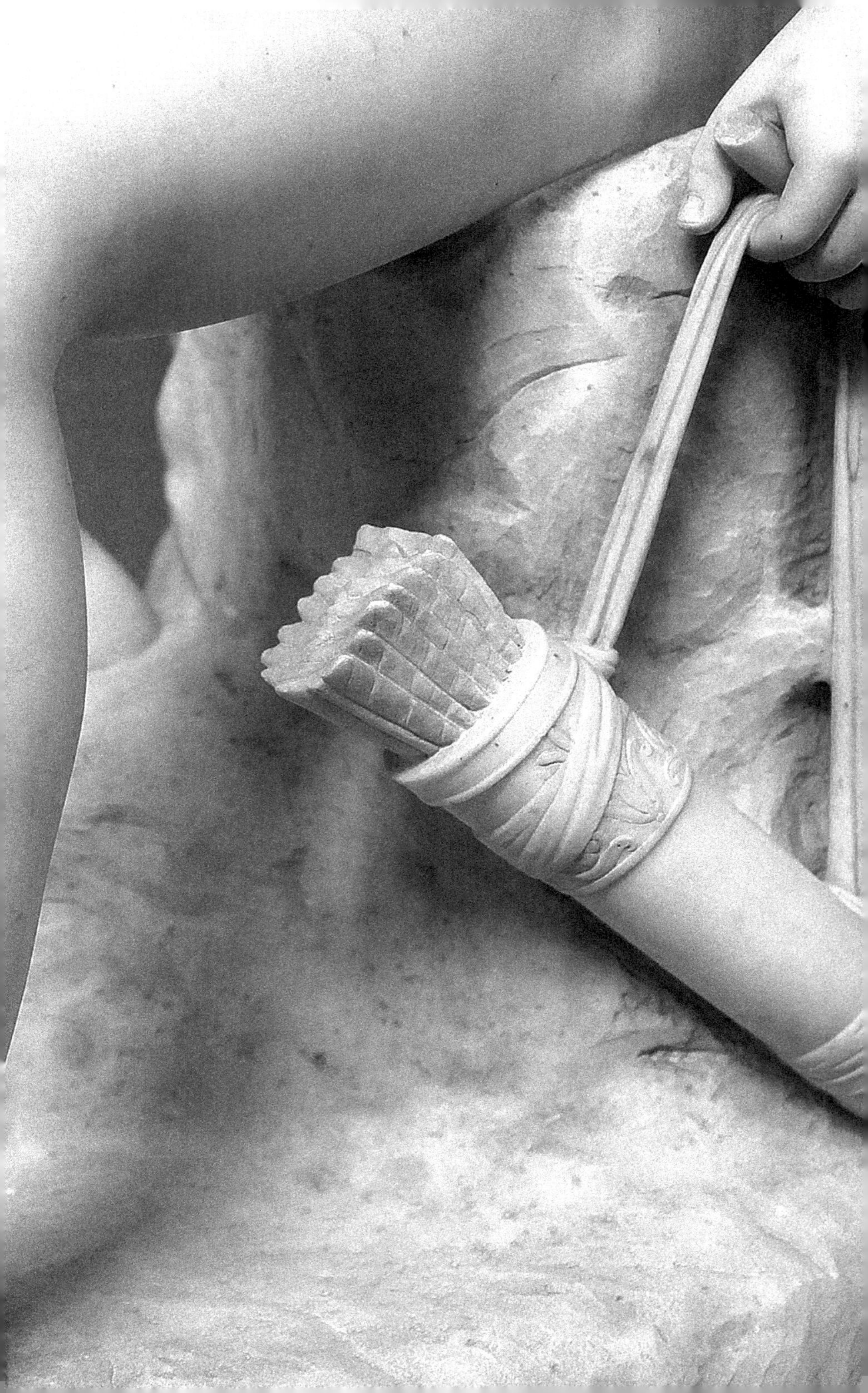

Love Counterattacks

Love defies boundaries
Will not be constrained
By mere social convention
Or memory of loss or pain
When it counterattacks
Unexpected once more

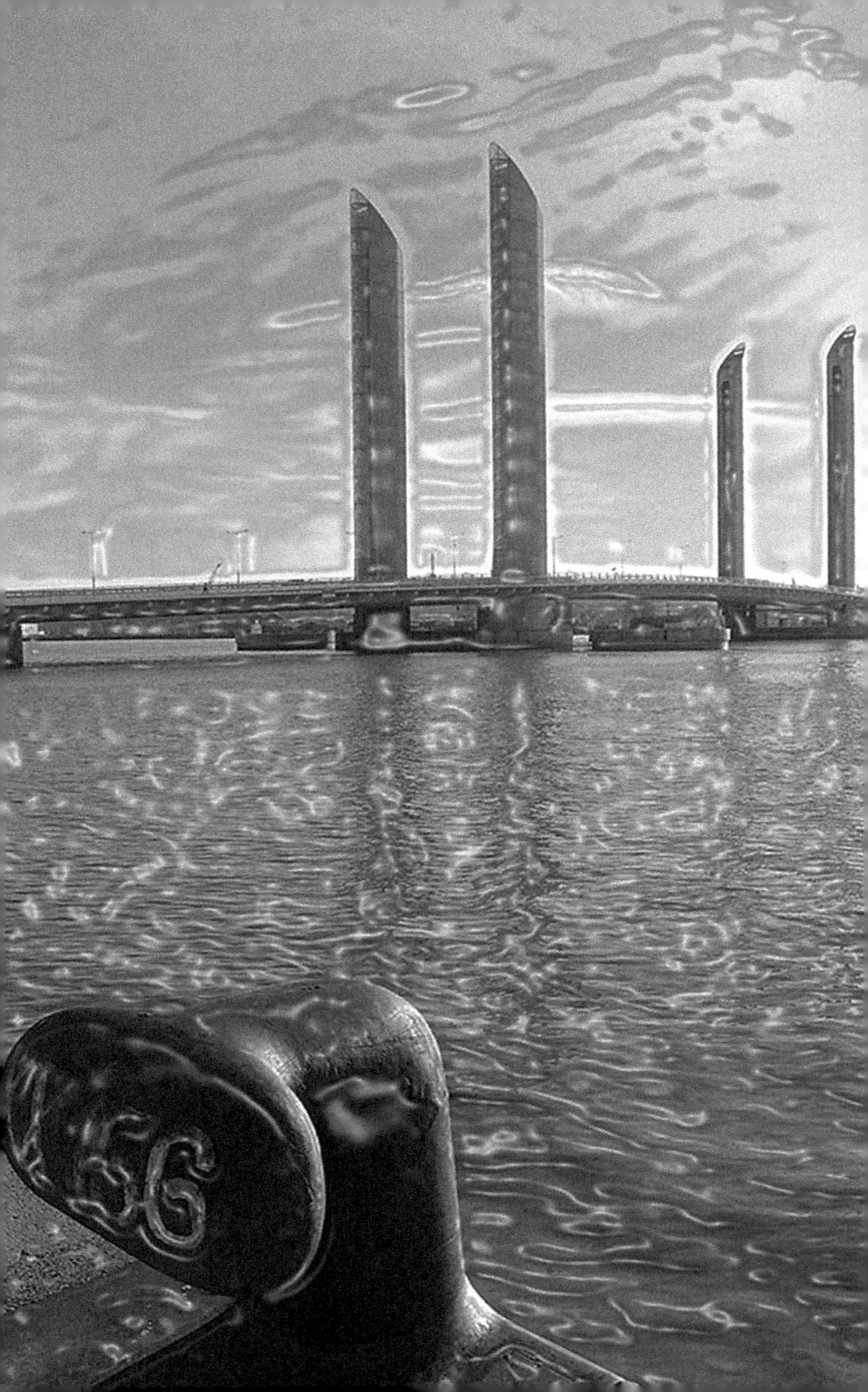
56

Digital Dilemma

Look up from your phone

It's a beautiful day

Out here

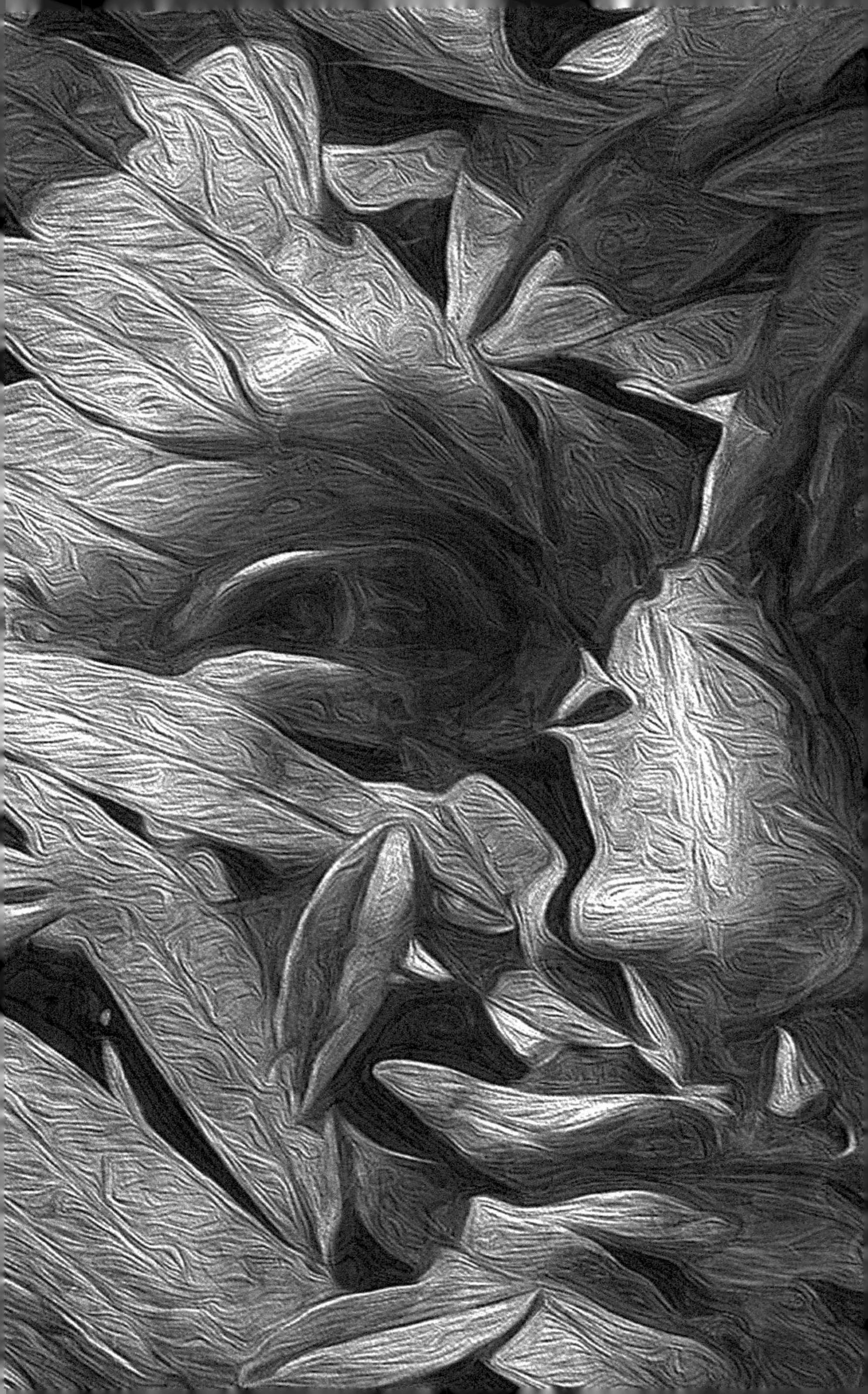

Inner Strength

Develop enough self-esteem

To see your strength

In the mirror

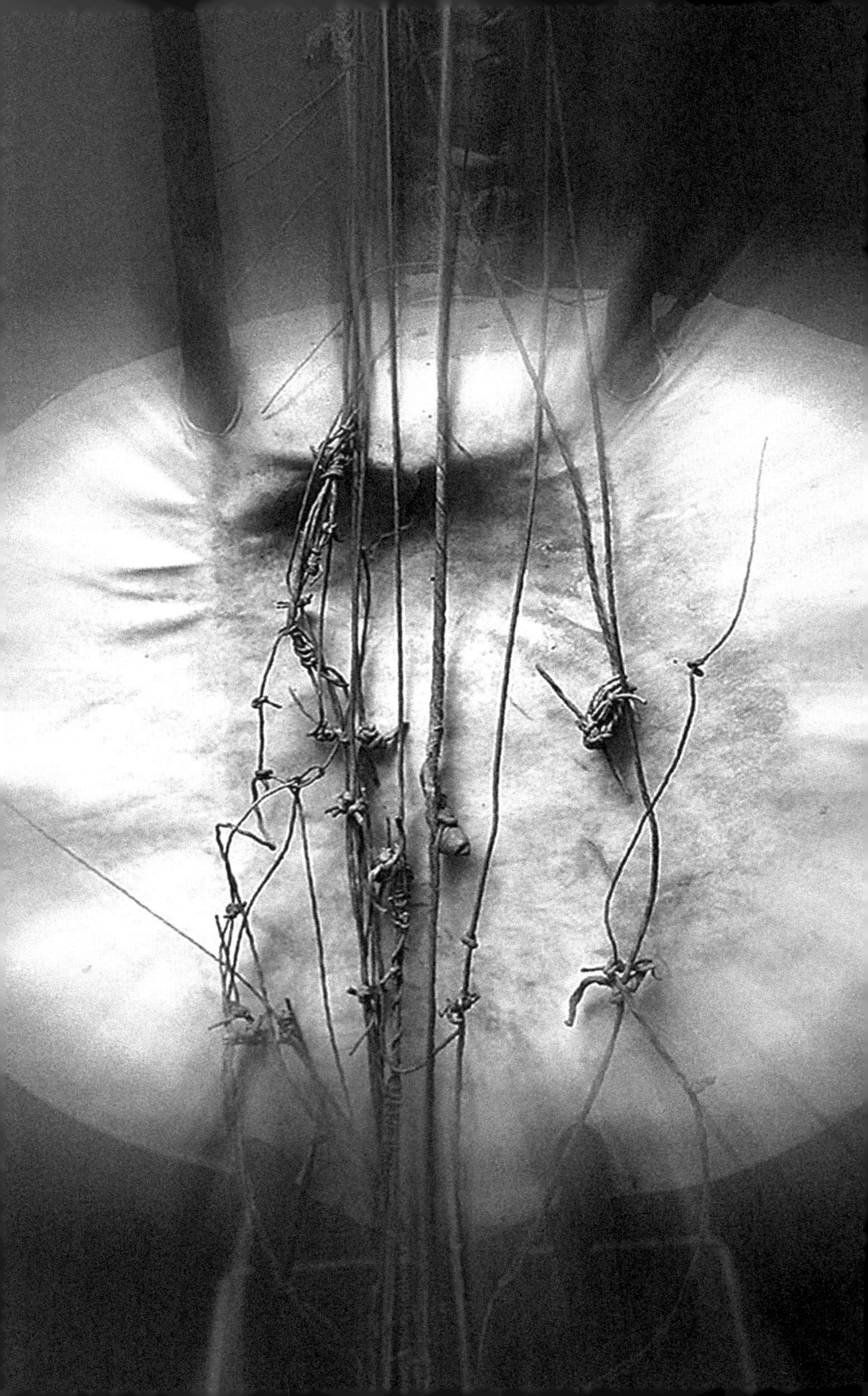

Goodbye Hello

Do not cling
To the grief of goodbyes
For farewells
And meetings
Are simply different sides
Of the same coin

And how can you embrace
The future
When you have not
Bidden farewell
To the past

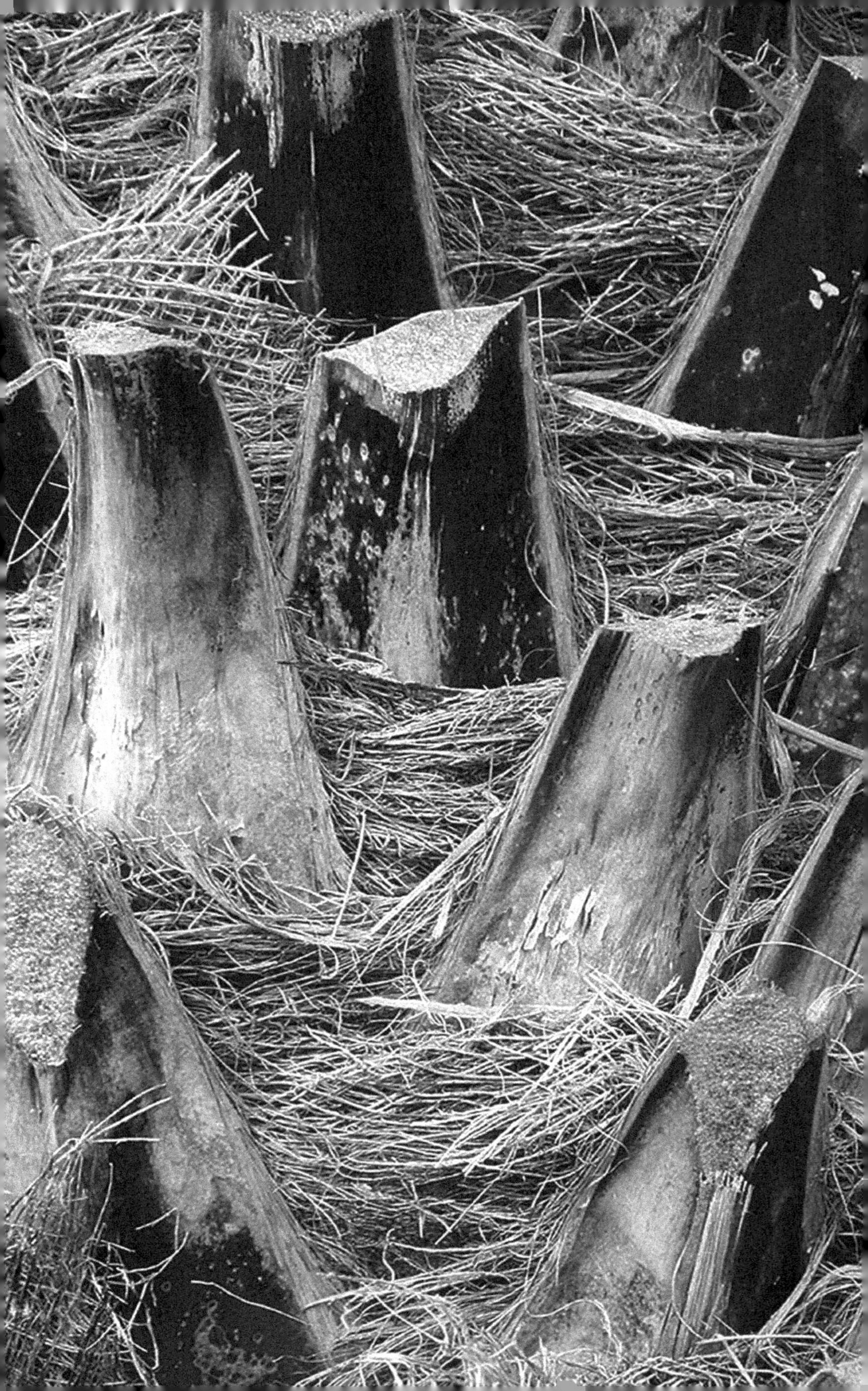

It's Your Life

Life is not simply
A collective endeavour
It remains intensely personal
And each of us
Finds the life
That we have gone looking for

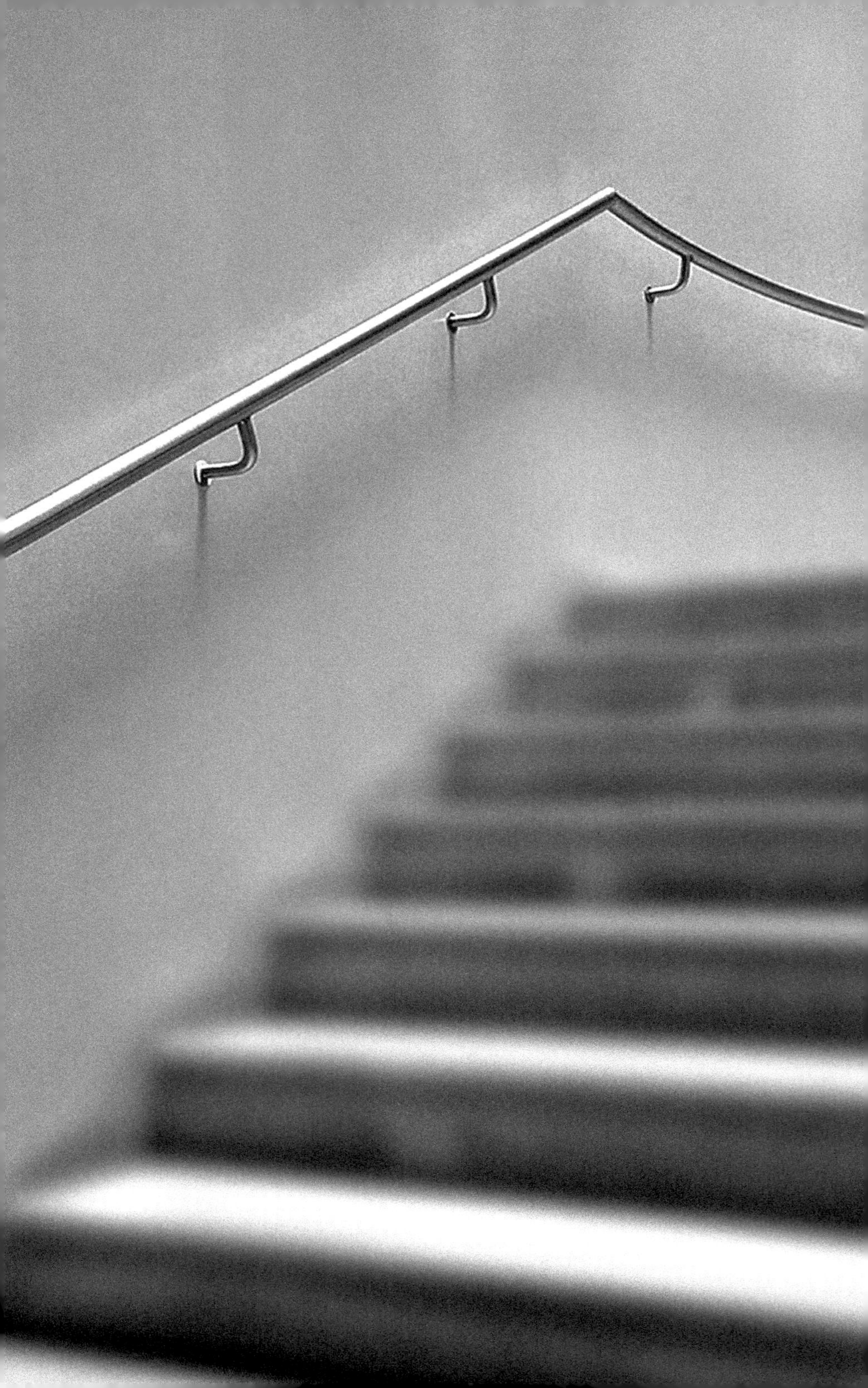

Virtual Lives

Step outside
Your digital world
Of fake perfection,
Loneliness and pretence

You might find
A life worth living

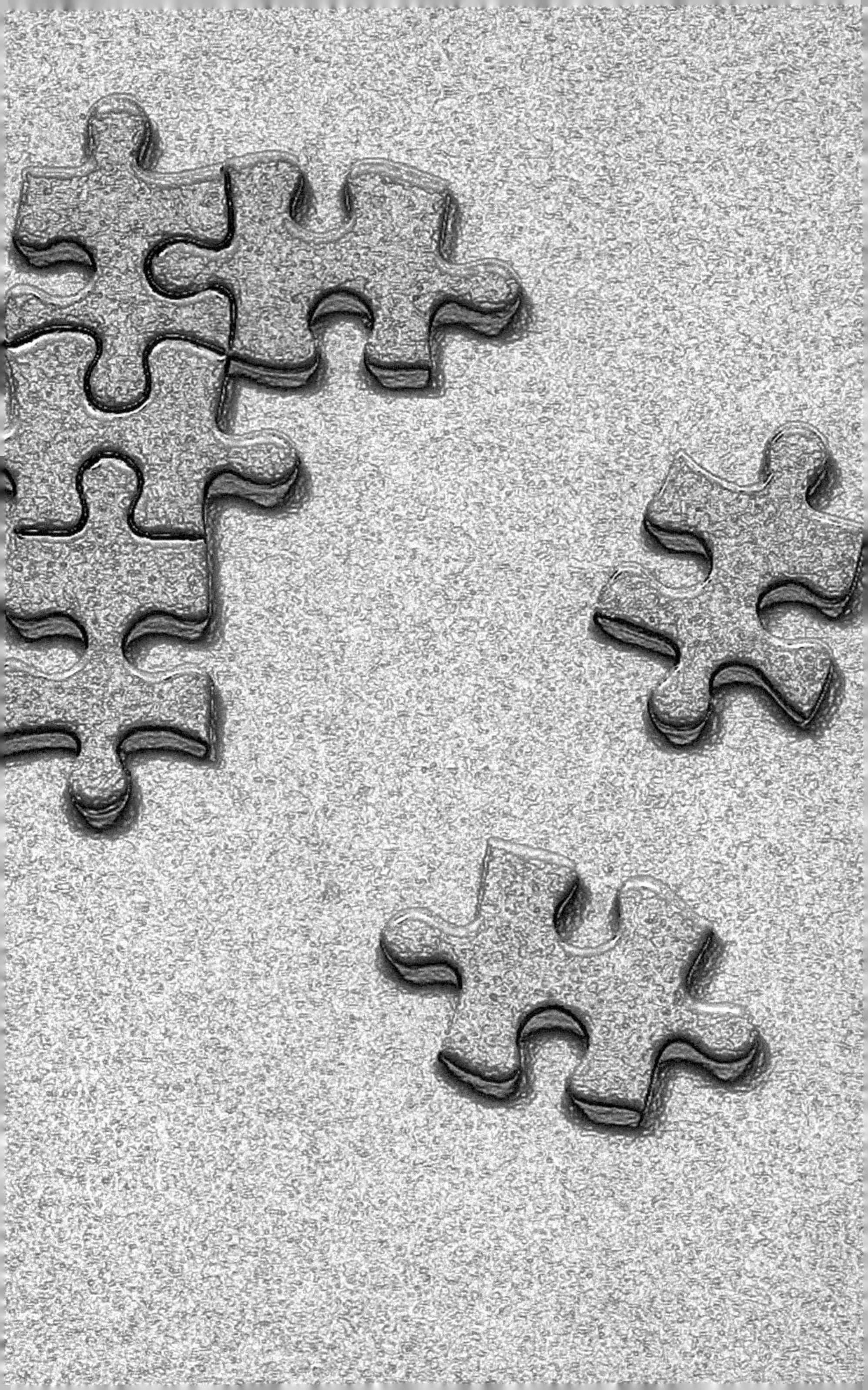

Picking up the Pieces

At some time
We all fall from grace
Or wander far from our roots,
Our beliefs and ourselves

But it is how
You pick yourself up
And use that experience
That defines you.

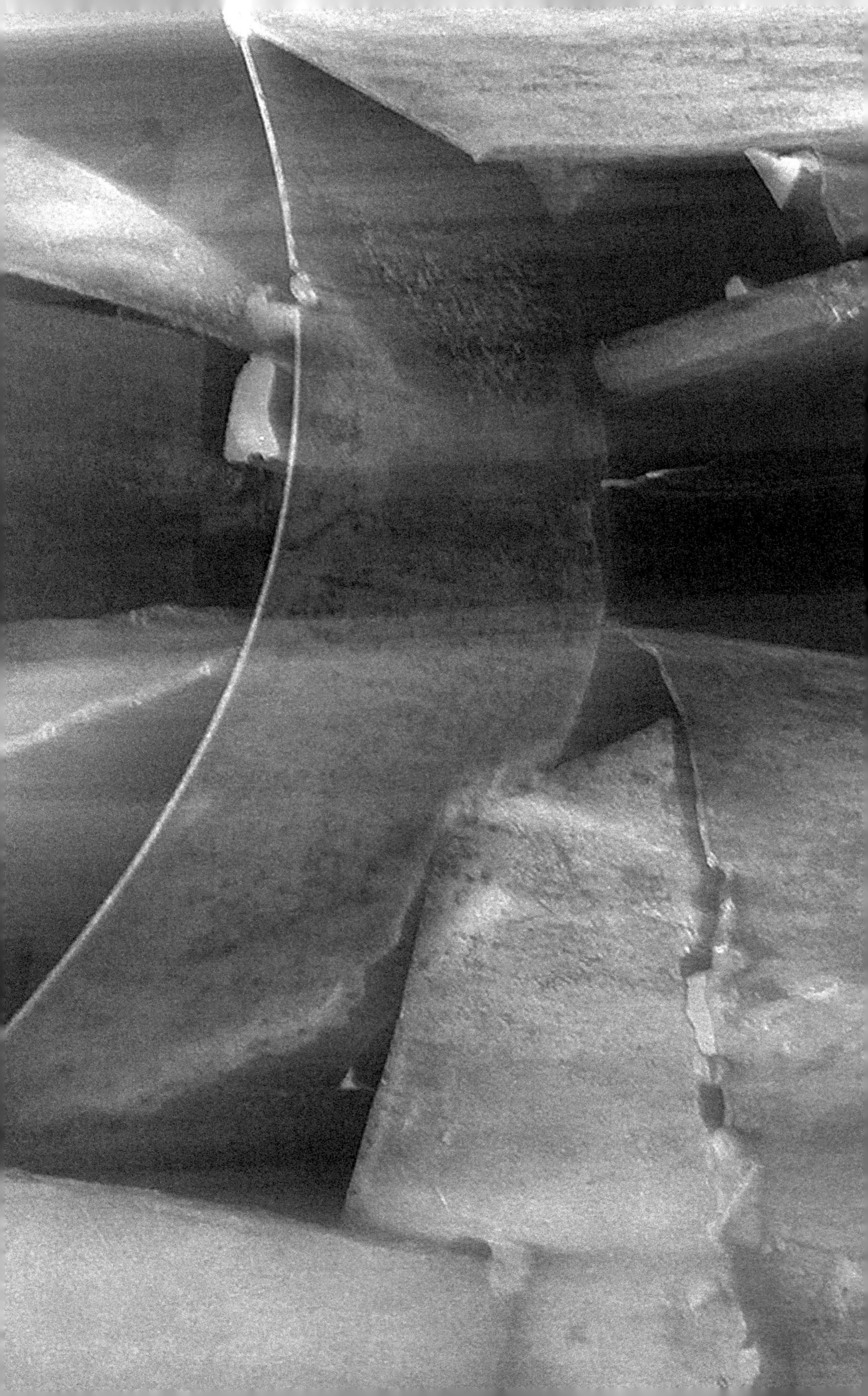

Experience

Concealed within

The despairing grasp

Of every problem

Is the precious gift

Of learning

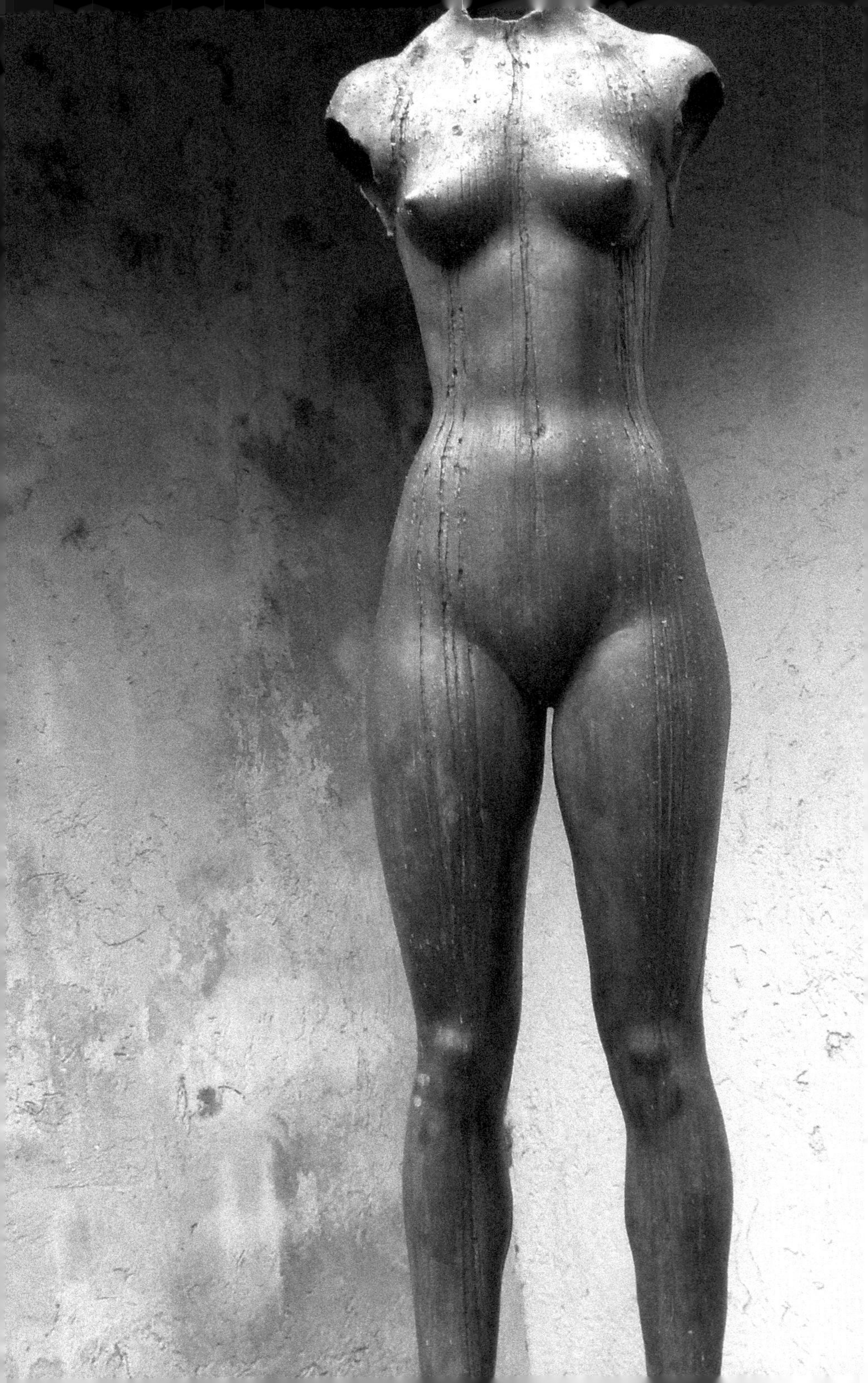

Secrets

Our darkest secrets,
Those we hold most dear,
Nurtured close to our hearts
And guarded jealously,
Hidden even from ourselves,
Are the ones most in need
Of spring cleaning
And resolution
Or banishment

Mountains

Oh mindful mountain
Speak silently
Amidst the chaos
And clamour
Unmoved, unbound

You sanctifying spirit
Protect and purify
My eternally searching soul
To bring me at last
To acceptance, hope
And peace

ONE

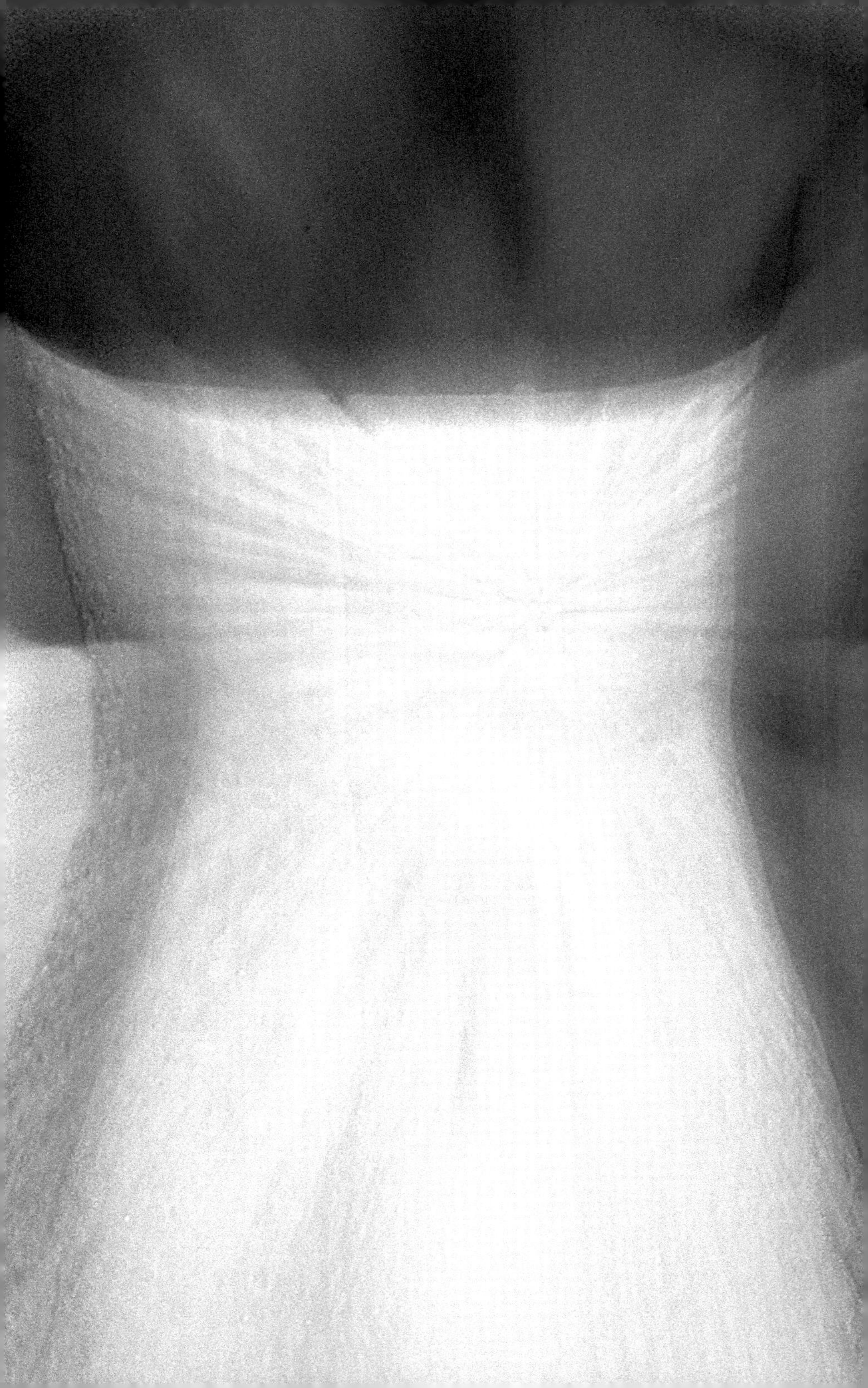

Love is the goal

Life is the journey

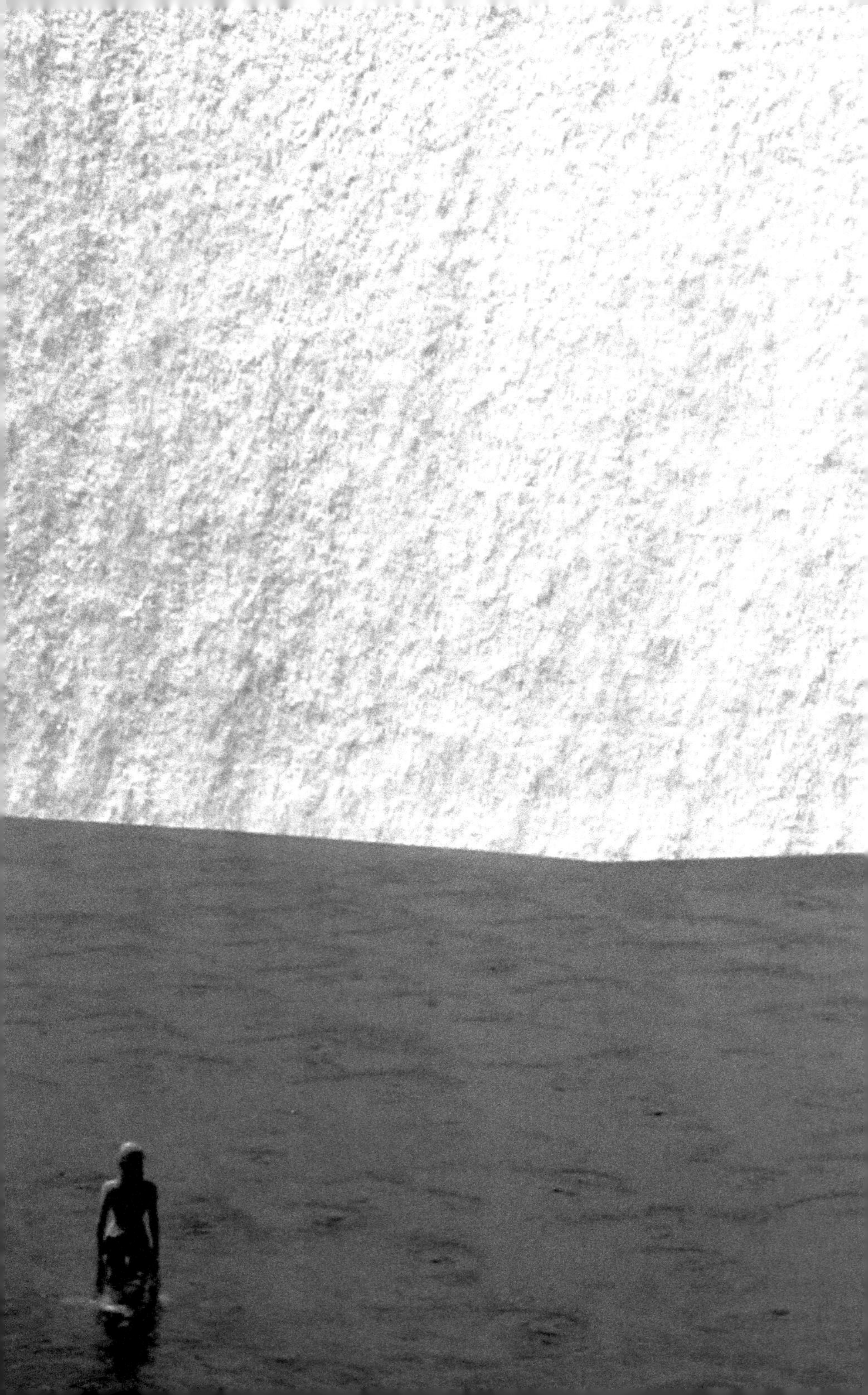

Embrace Love

When love calls you
Do not hesitate
Or doubt its intent
Just jump in
With all of your being
In supplication and desire
And disappear in its wonders

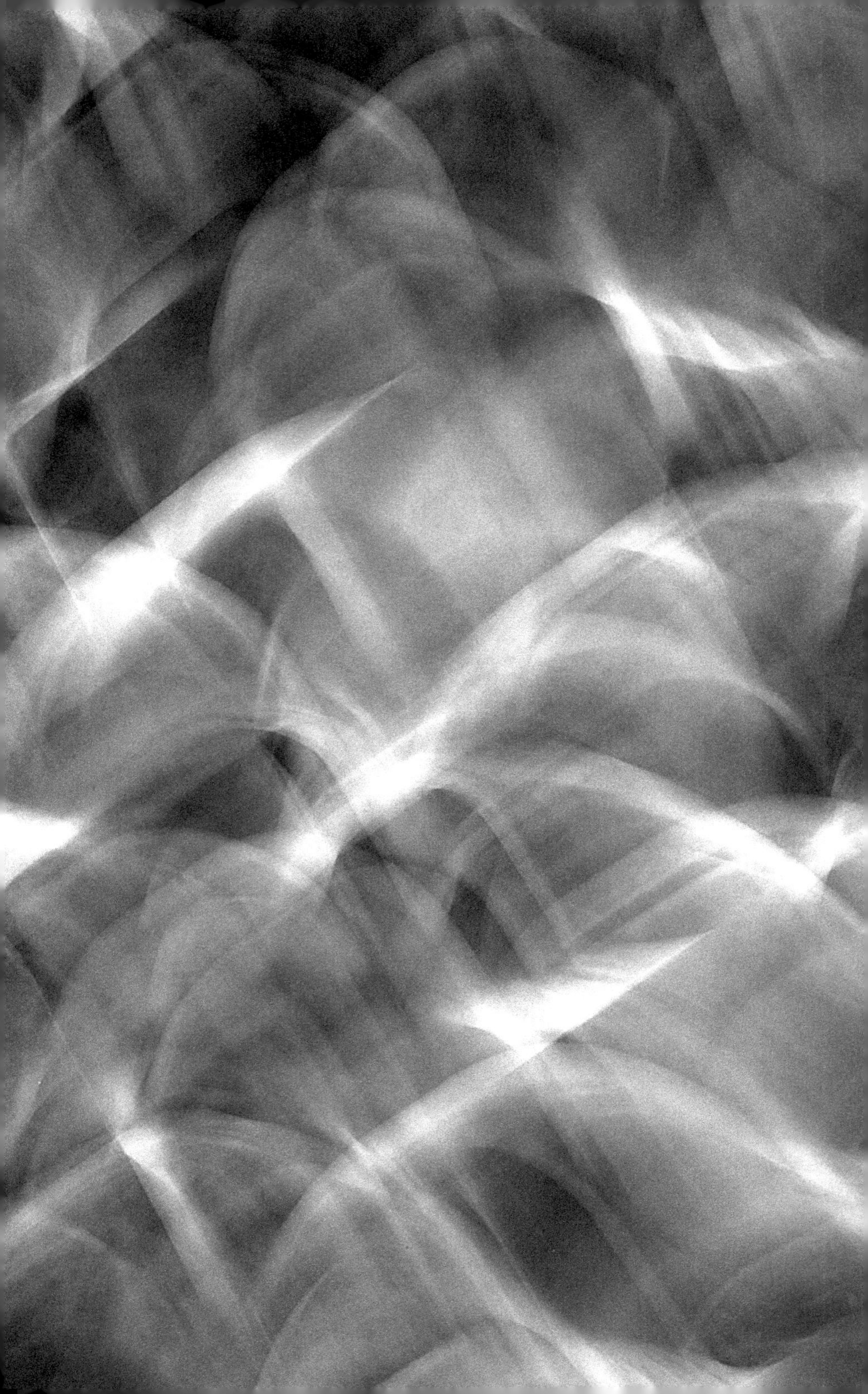

Love gives you Wings

On tender, unfamiliar wings

Take flight together now

Embrace the dawning love

With freshness and awe

And marvel in humble delight

As you discover that you too

Are worthy

Life's Journey

I will follow you

All the days

Of our lives

With open heart

And joyful step

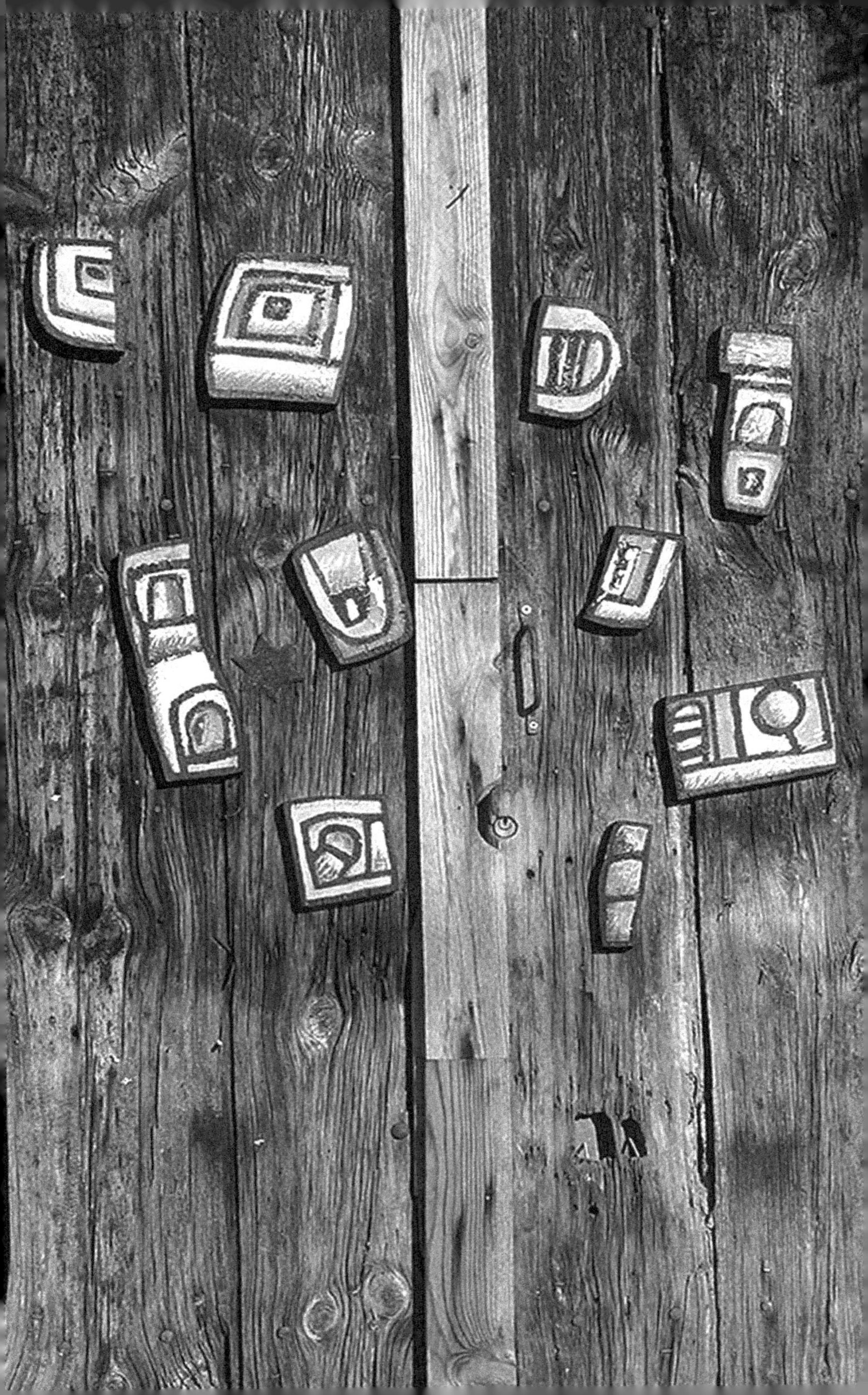

Deserving Love

Do you love yourself enough,

To love me

As we deserve?

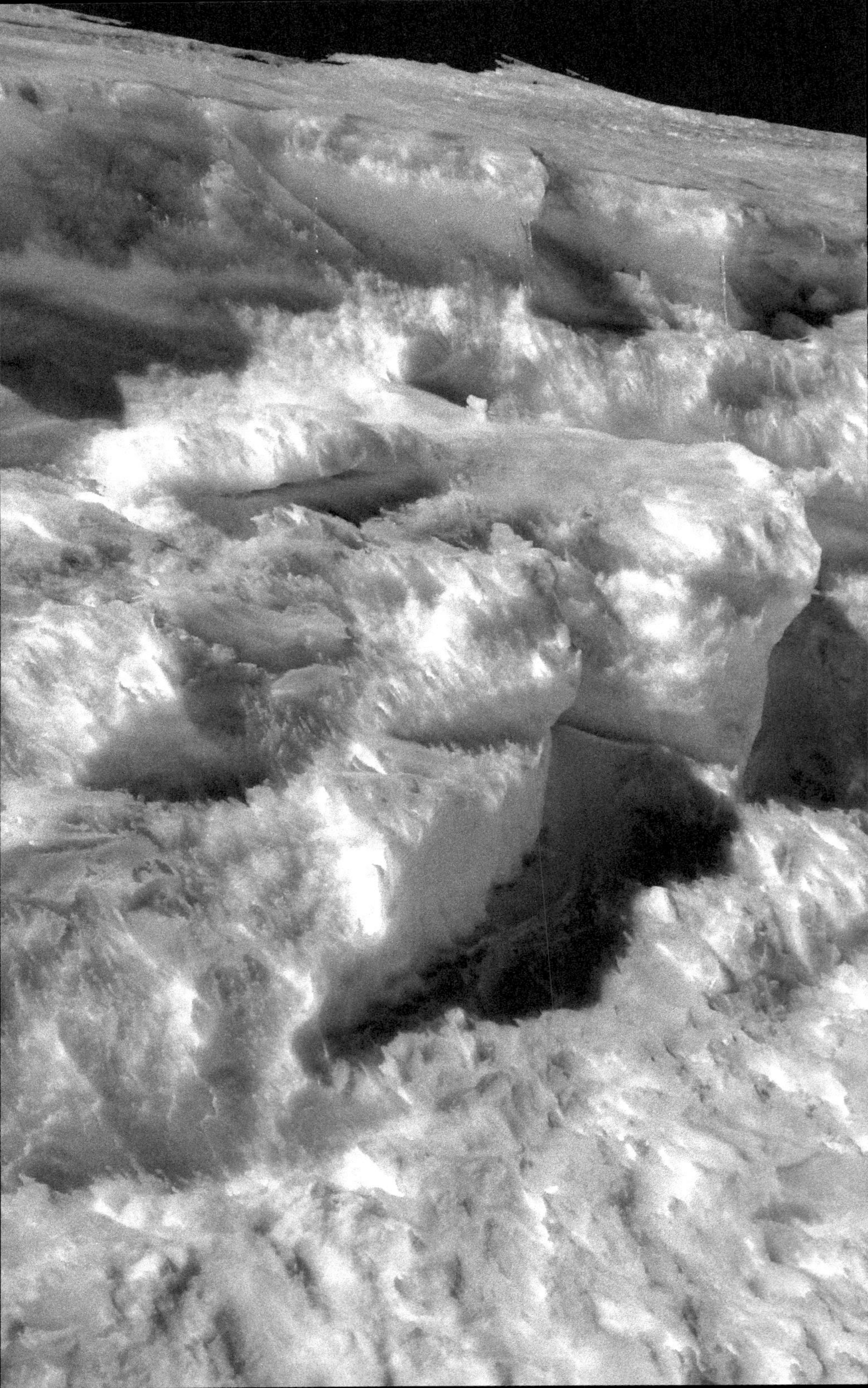

Dancing in the Snow

I watch you dancing
In the snow
And know at once
That you are all
That I will ever need
In this life
And the next

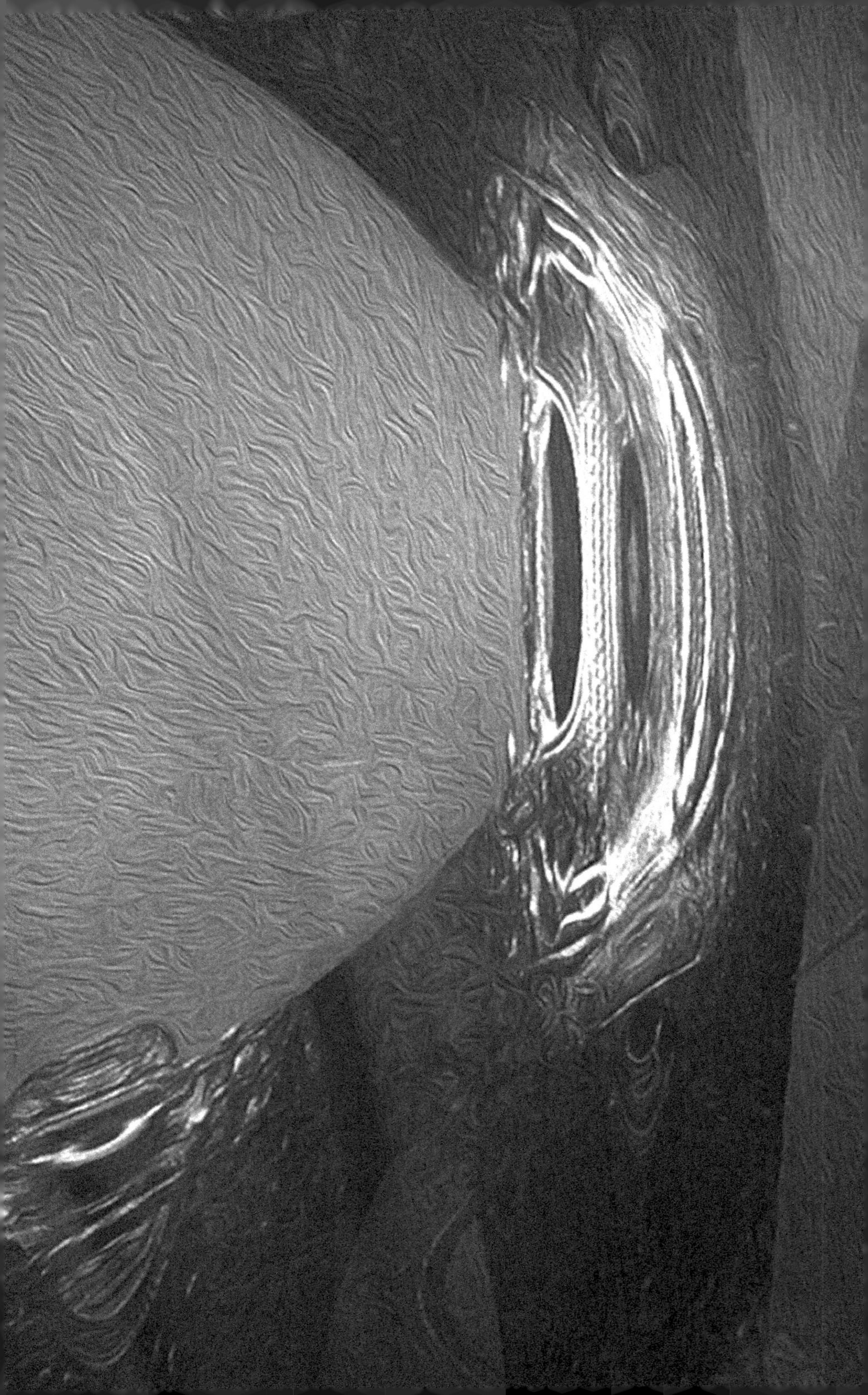

Yin Yang

The two
That become one
And the one
That is two

Lovers entwined
United unto themselves
Yet half
Of a larger whole

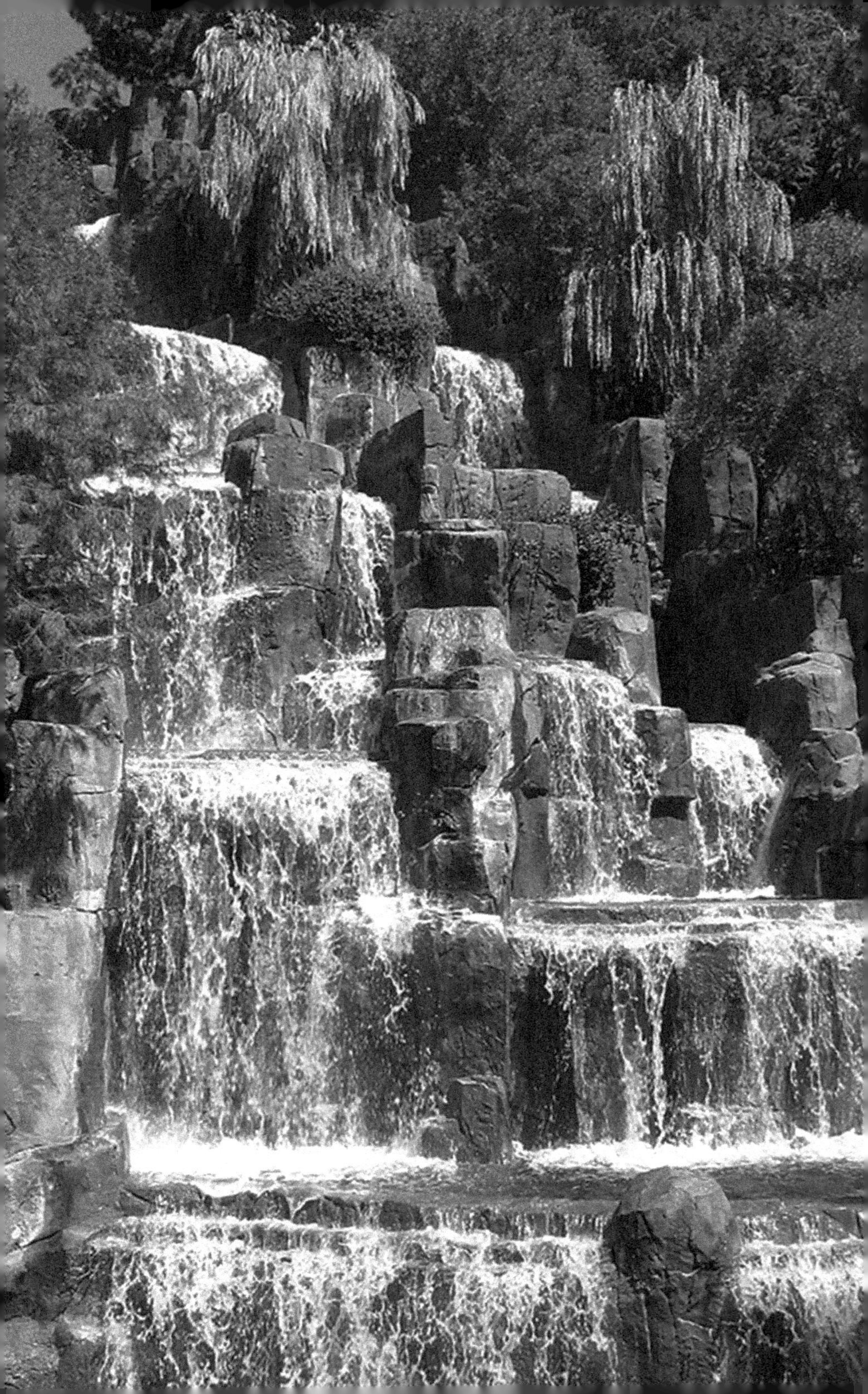

It Starts with One

Love is a boundless stair

It starts

With one person

One step along the way

And ends

With totality

Total abandonment

Or oblivion

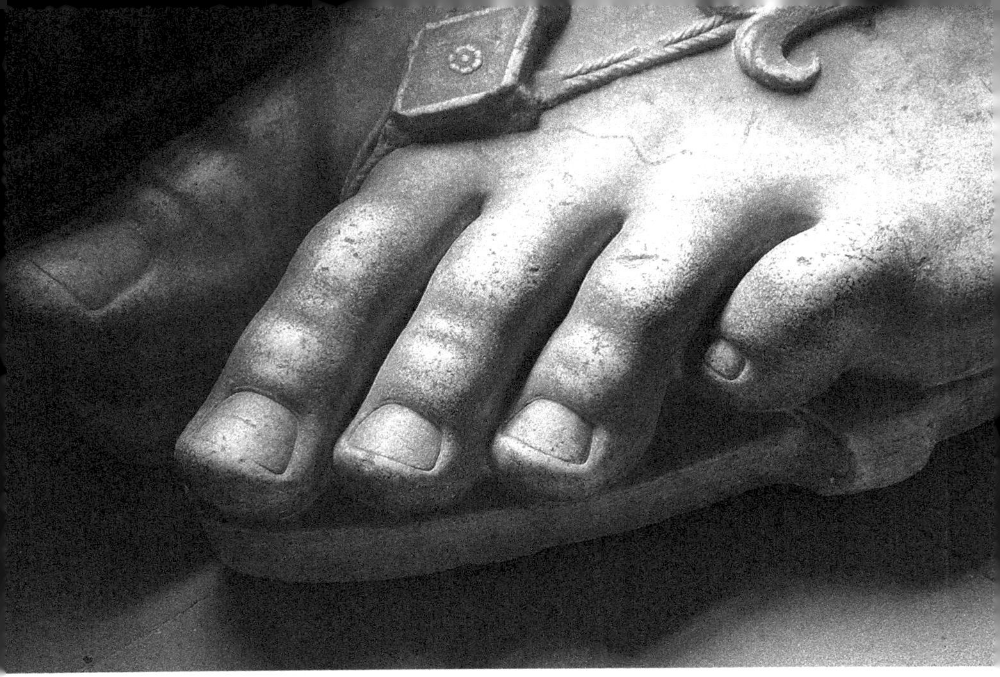

Sacred Steps

So step
By sacred step
In glorious ascension
We tread
This newfound path
Of you and I

Seeking fulfilment
And a higher union
As soul explores soul
And all things
Become possible

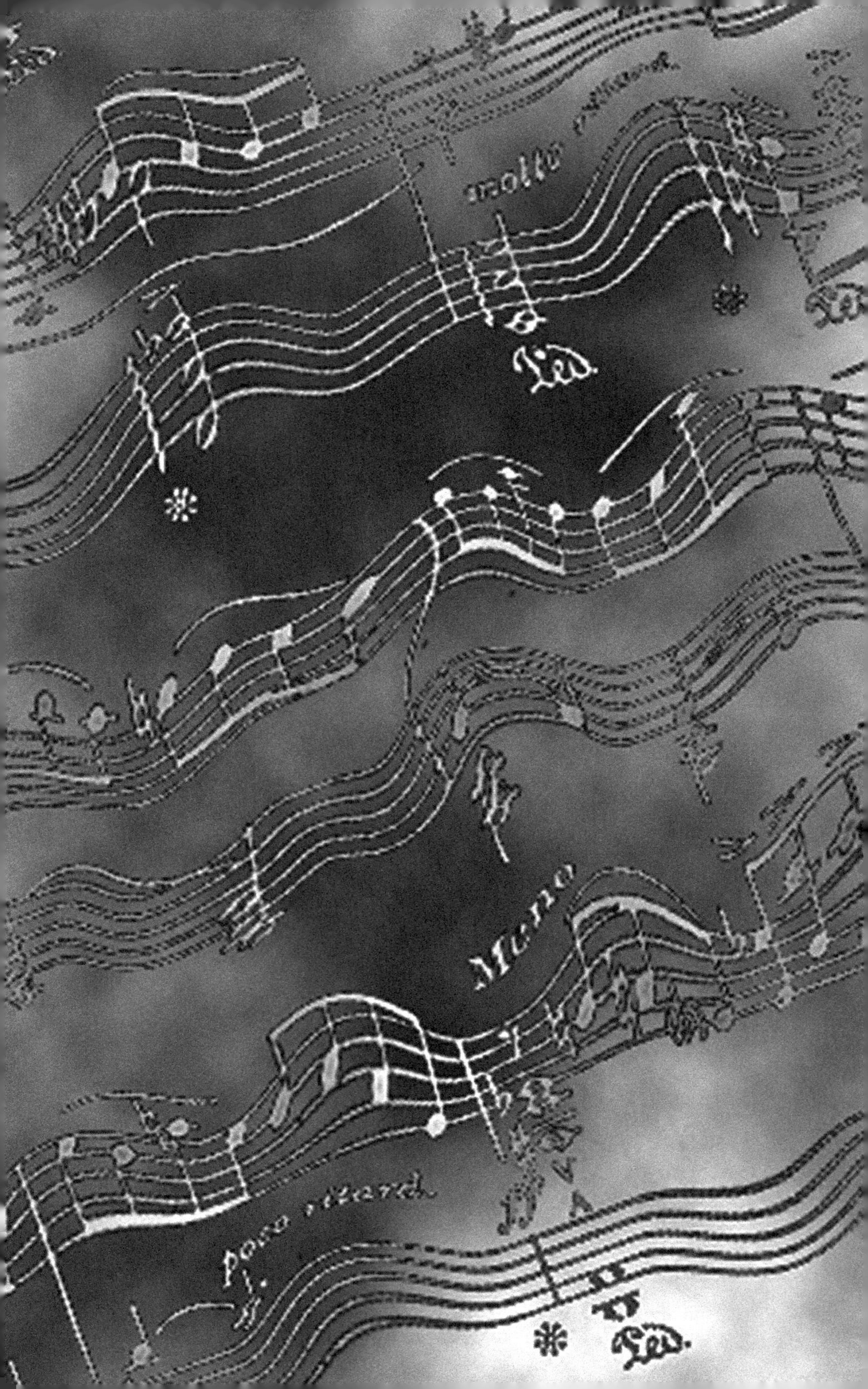

molto ritard.
Ped.
Meno
poco ritard.
Ped.

Heart Song

Everyone has a song

That resonates deep within their heart

Stirring their soul

To unbridled flight

Find your song

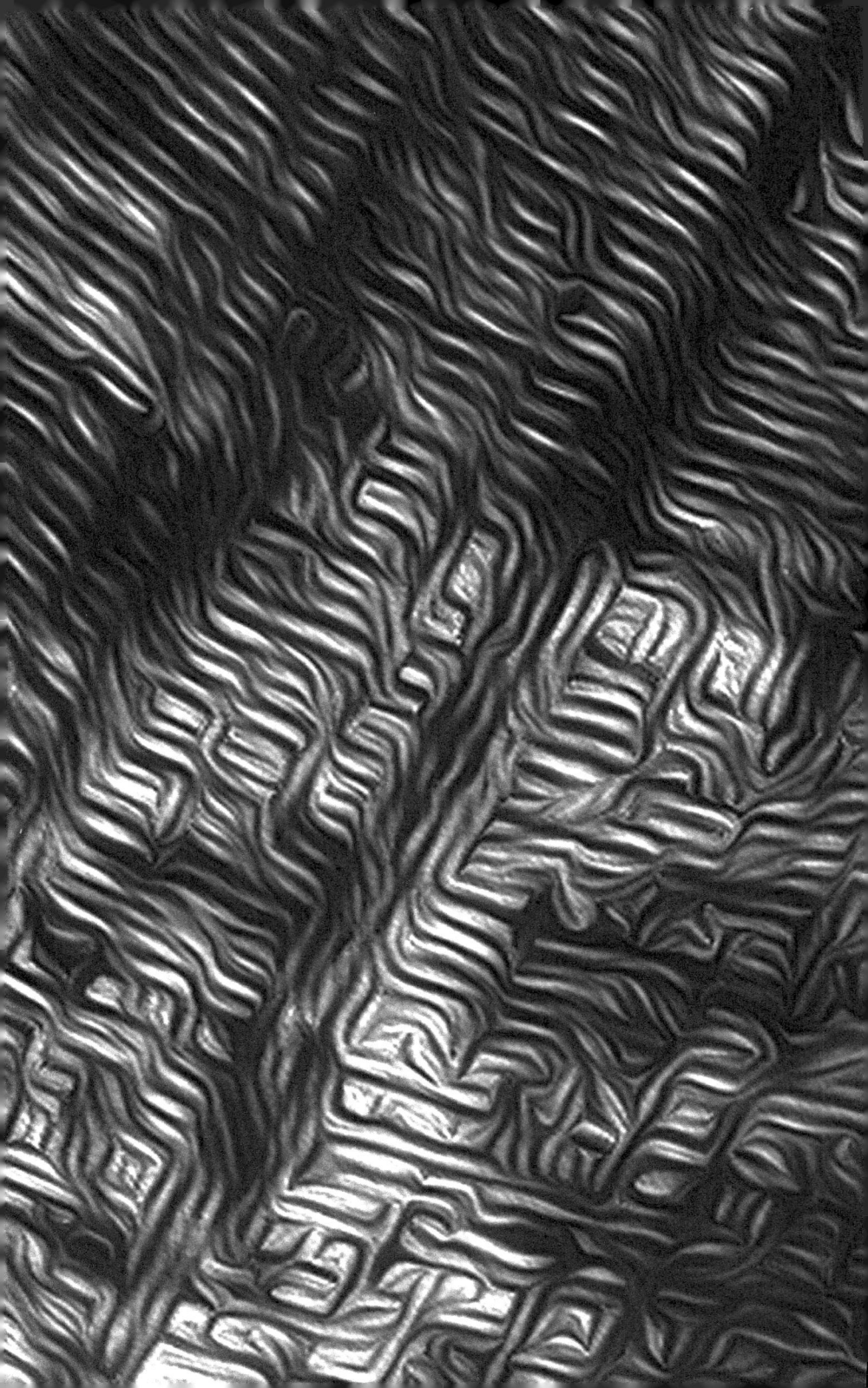

Love Requires Effort

You both deserve better

Work harder

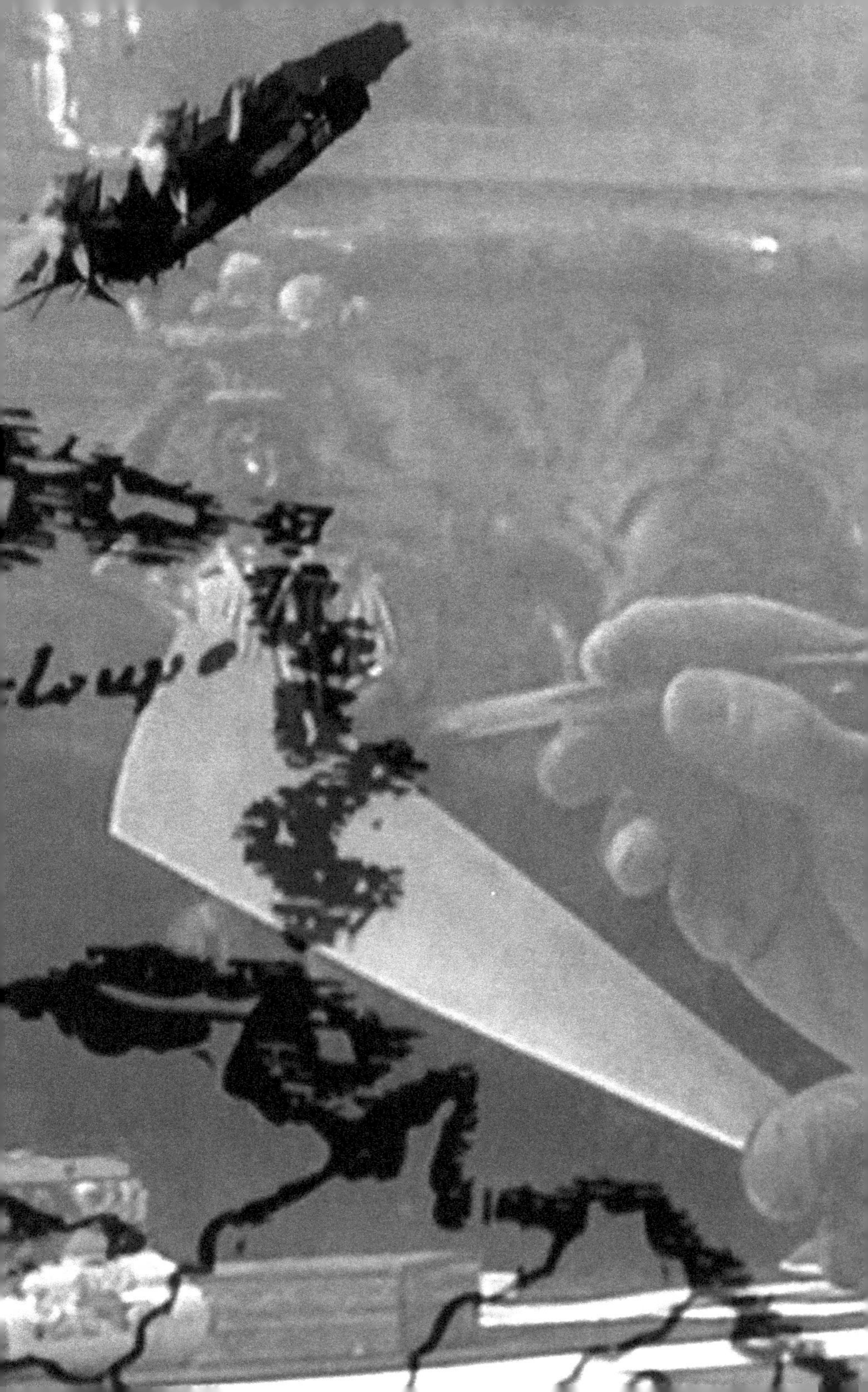

Trust your Heart

Trust the story
Not the storyteller

Trust the song
Not the singer

Trust the poem
Not the poet

Trust your heart
To lead you through the night

Tomorrow is a New Day

Love is given eyes
To cast aside the gloom
And despair of the past
And to pierce
The shifting shadows
Of the future self
And light the way
To a new tomorrow

Be True to Yourself

Be true to yourself

It is the only thing
That counts

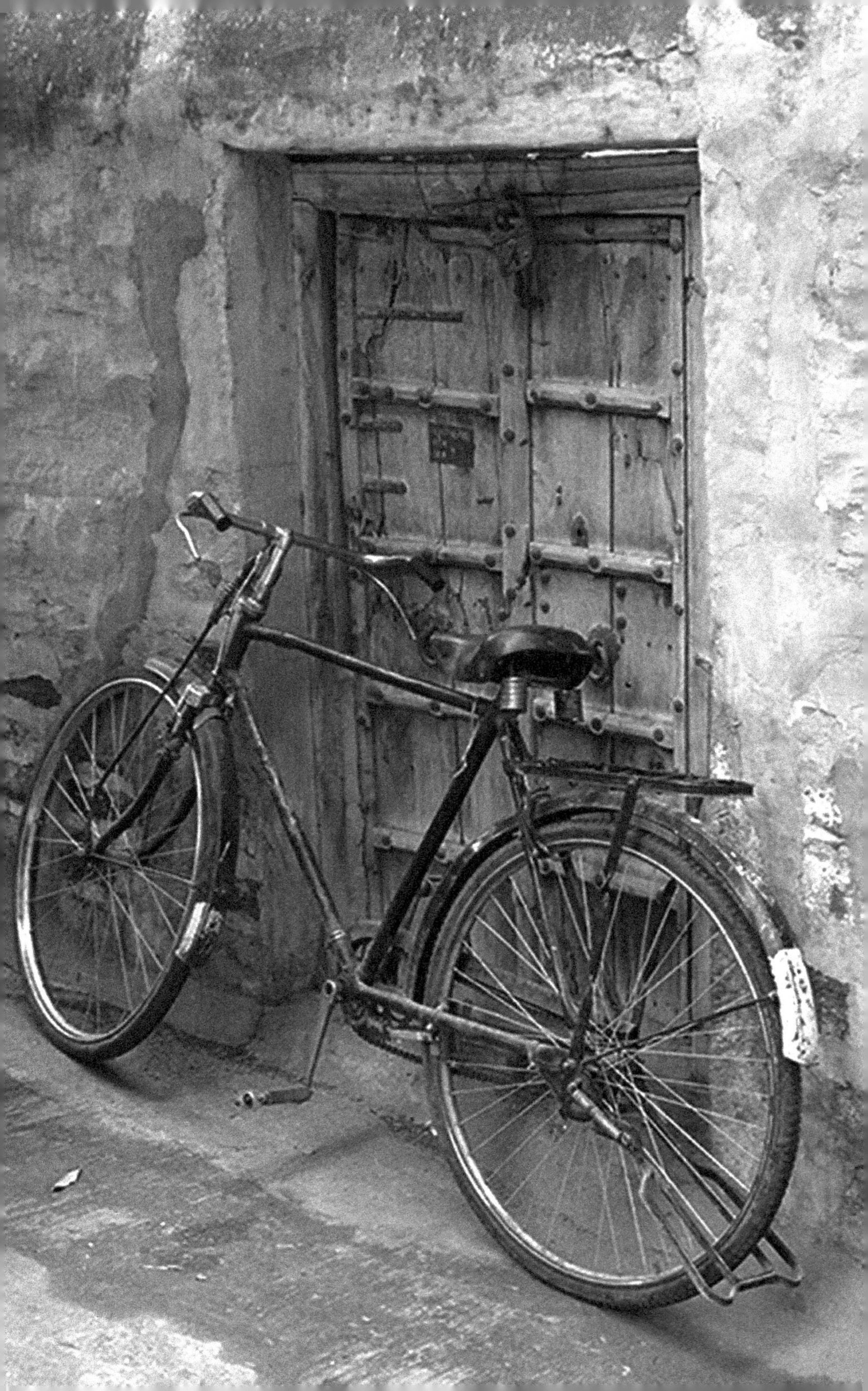

Life is the Journey

There is nothing,

No emotion

Or action,

No desire

Nor distraction,

That is not

Part of the way

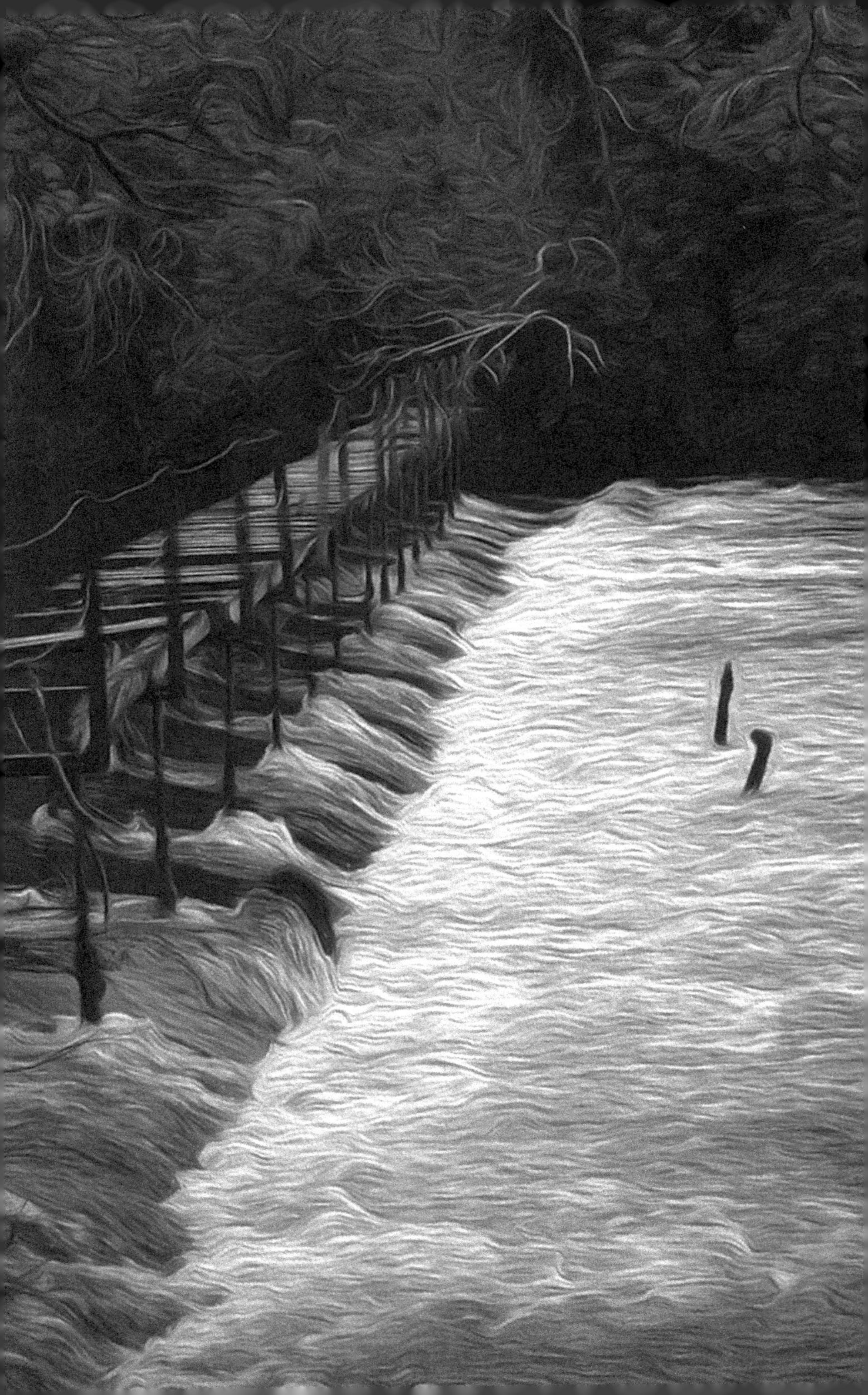

Dive in

Life is the untamed river,
Searching its way
Unerringly to the sea,
You can either fight against it,
Straining against the current,
Exhausting every part of you,
Mind, body and soul,
Or float within its eager grasp
To see where it takes you.

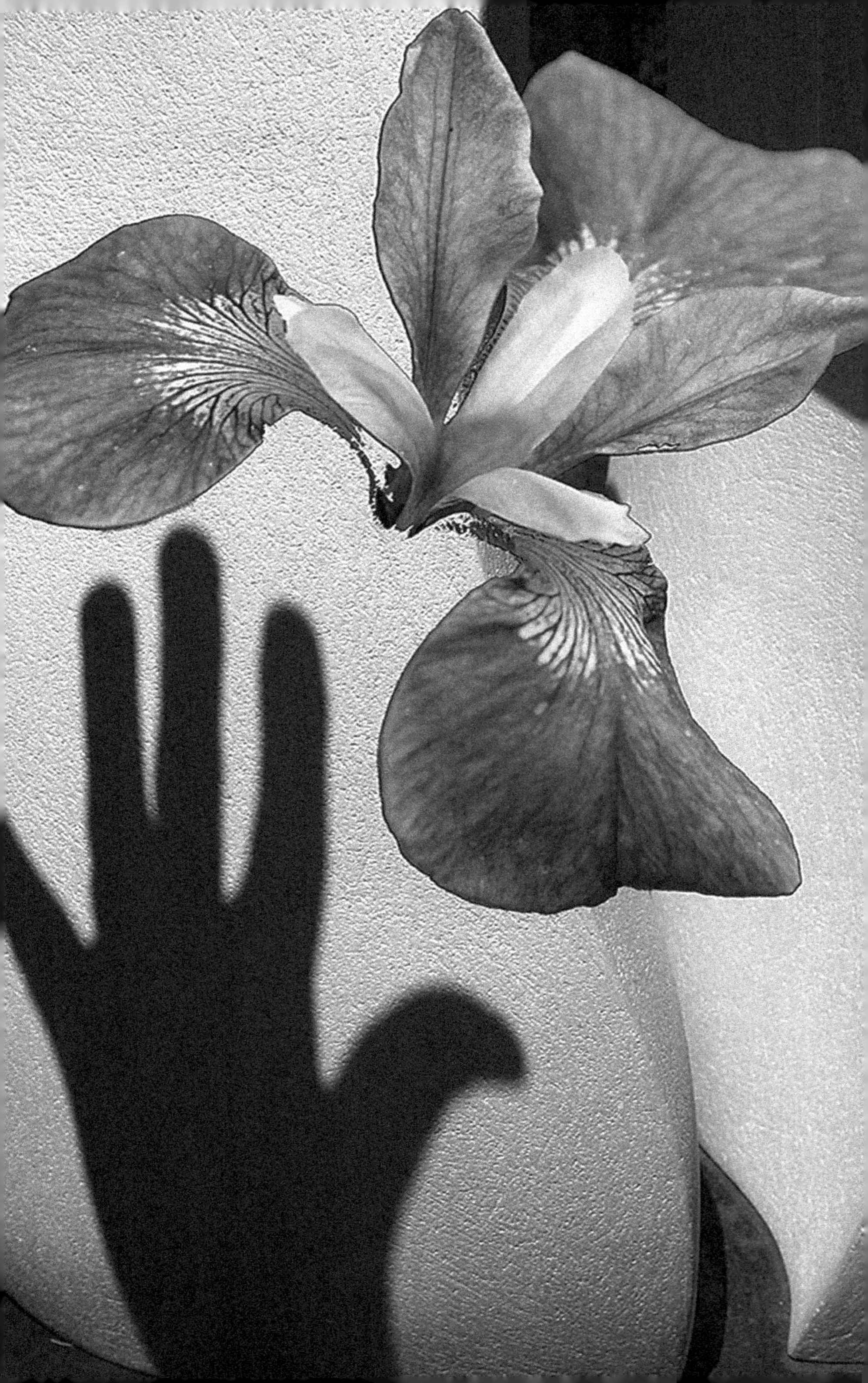

Open Hand

What undiminshed hope

Rests in the simple gesture

Of an outstretched hand

First Love

Watching you stand by me
In blessed union
Doubts melt softly away
Each breath an awakening
A new possibility
Of first love
In Eden's dawning light

Exuberant Existence

Let yourself know
The glory of life
The sheer, joyful exuberance
And fulfilment
Of existence
Is yours
If you take that step
And trust your heart
To guide your footsteps
Into the unknown

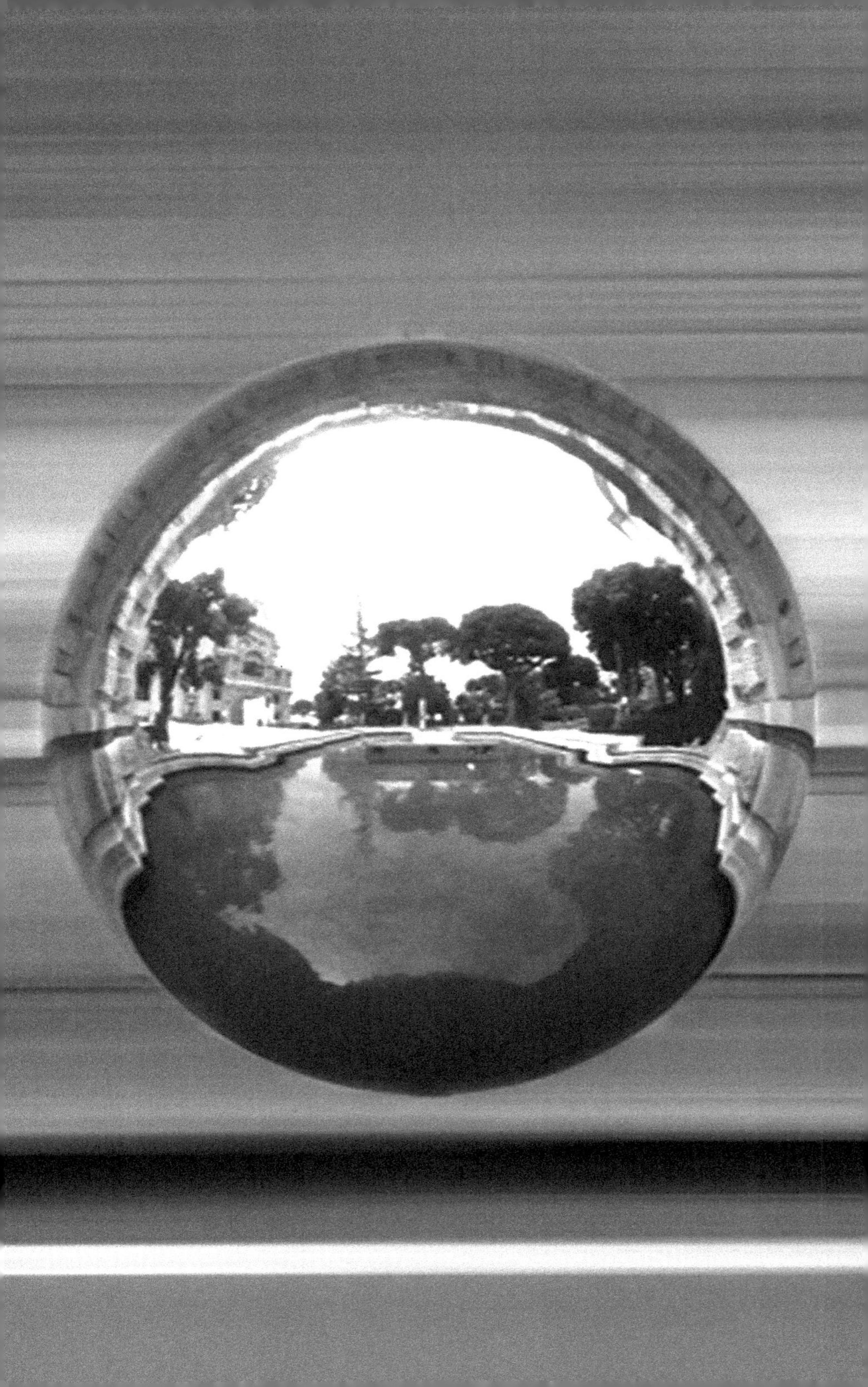

Life is a Mirror

The mirror of life
Reflects your troubled face
Though it be dusty
And stained with travel
The detritus of life

Be friendly
Be open
Be without judgement
And all of life
Will reflect that warm
And welcoming glow
To embrace you
And clear the mirror
Of clouds and doubt

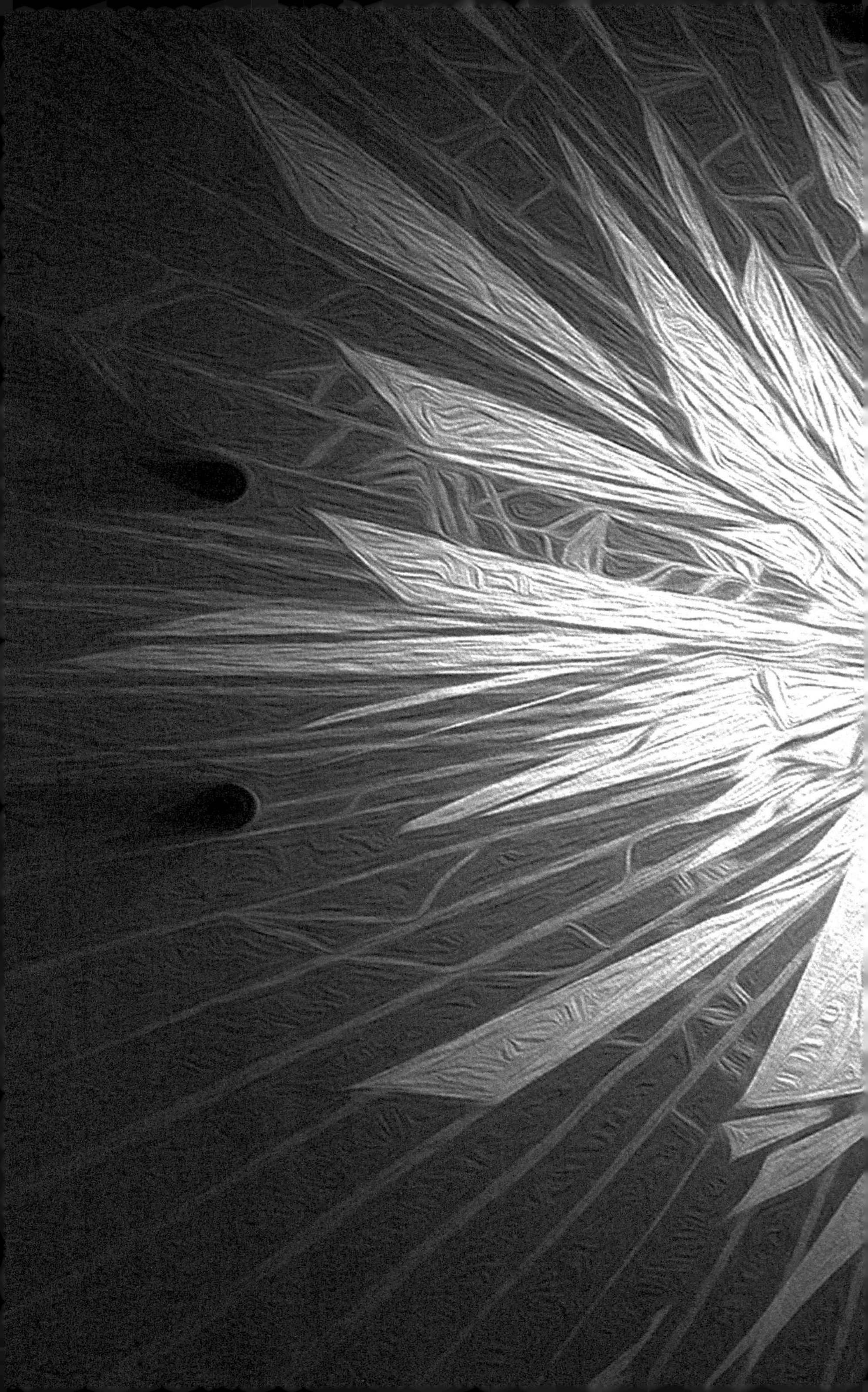

Unpredictable Love

Love strikes

When unexpected

And often

When unwanted

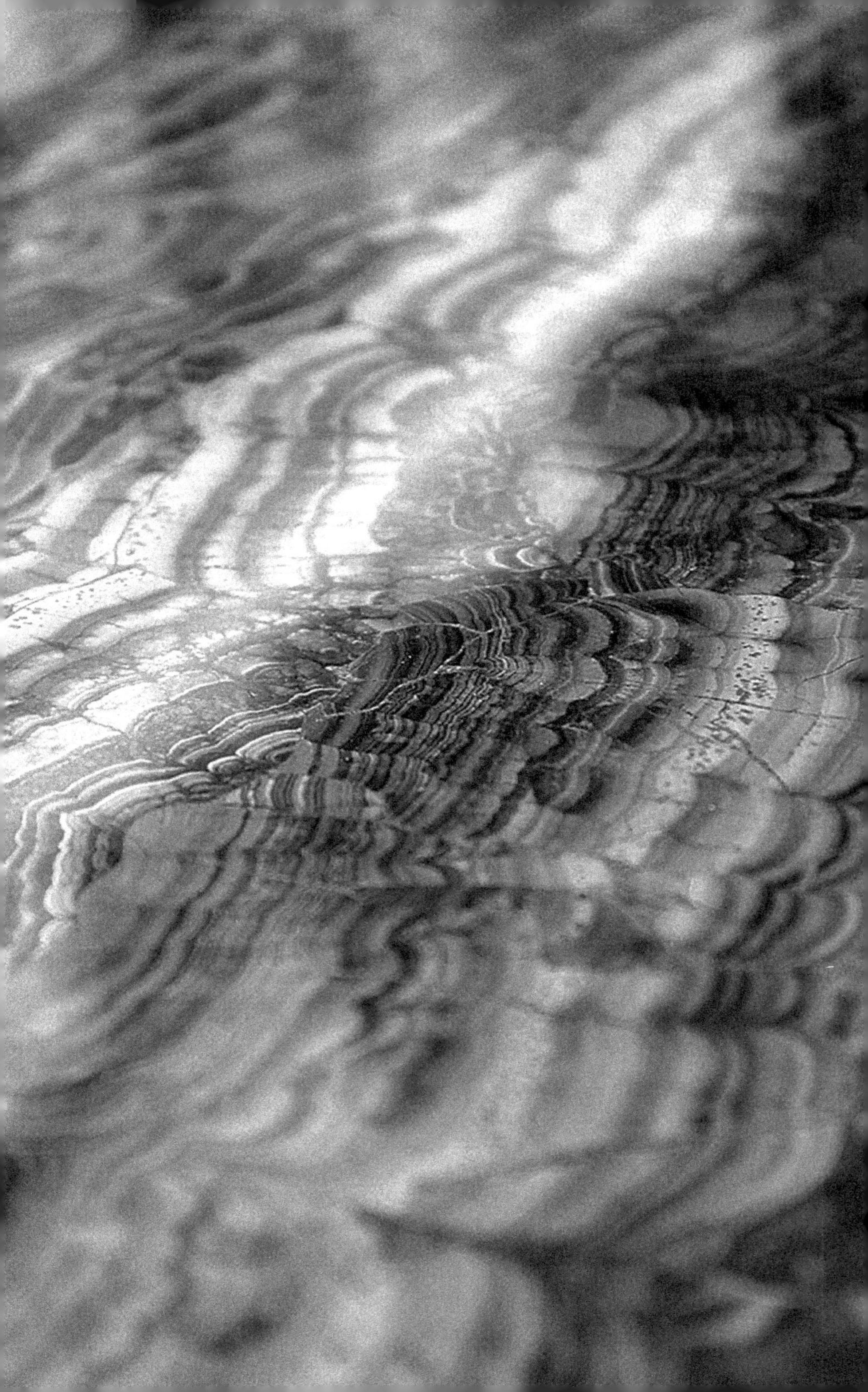

Live in Wonder

Do not live in knowledge
And fear of past wrongs
And dark intentions

Live in wonder
For life is surprising

Every moment is new
Seize it!

You have nothing to lose
And you may gain everything

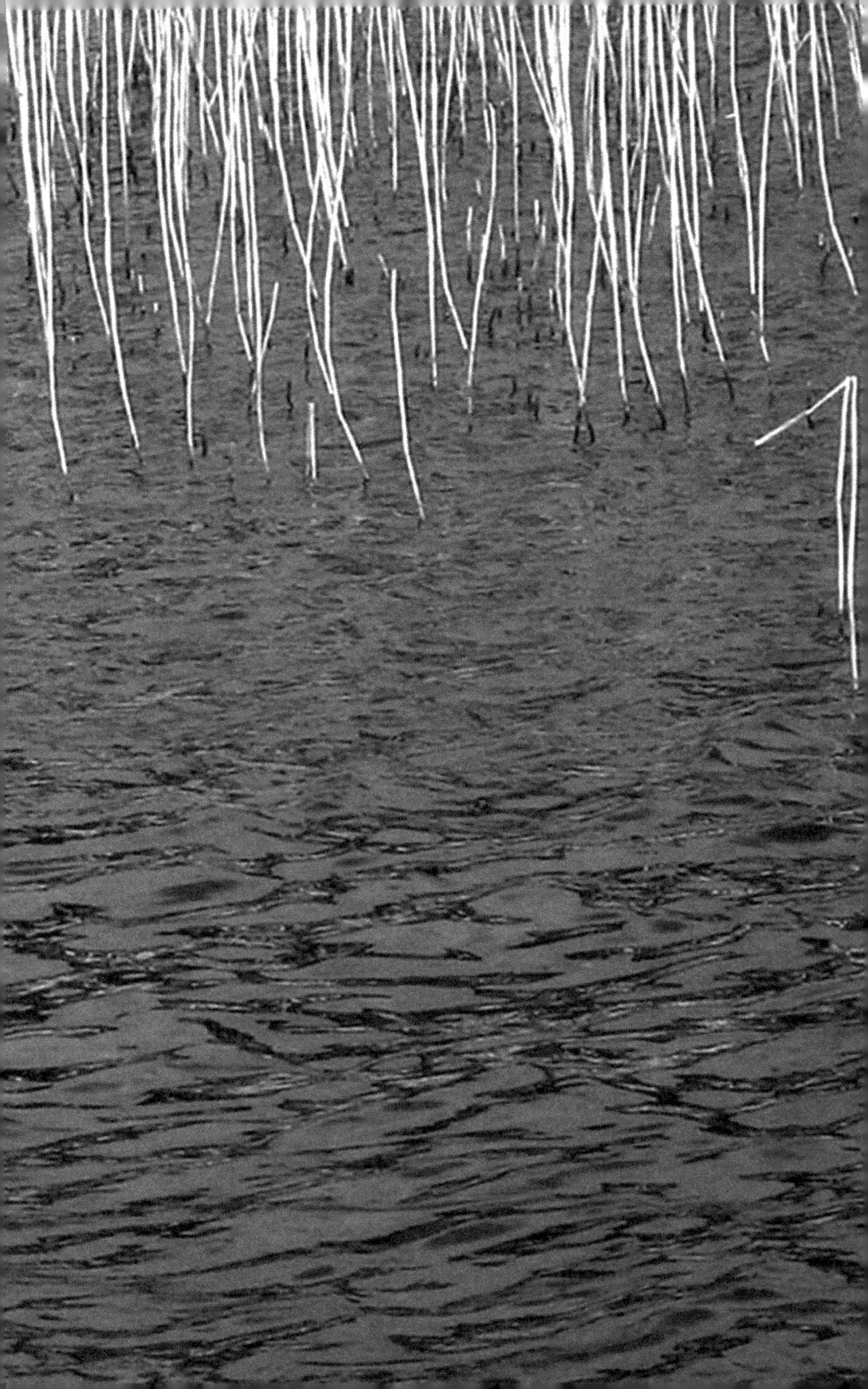

No Final Destination

Life is unconstrained
Directionless
There is no final destination

So rejoice in everything
Despite all that you
Might encounter along the way

There is no place
Where the road ends

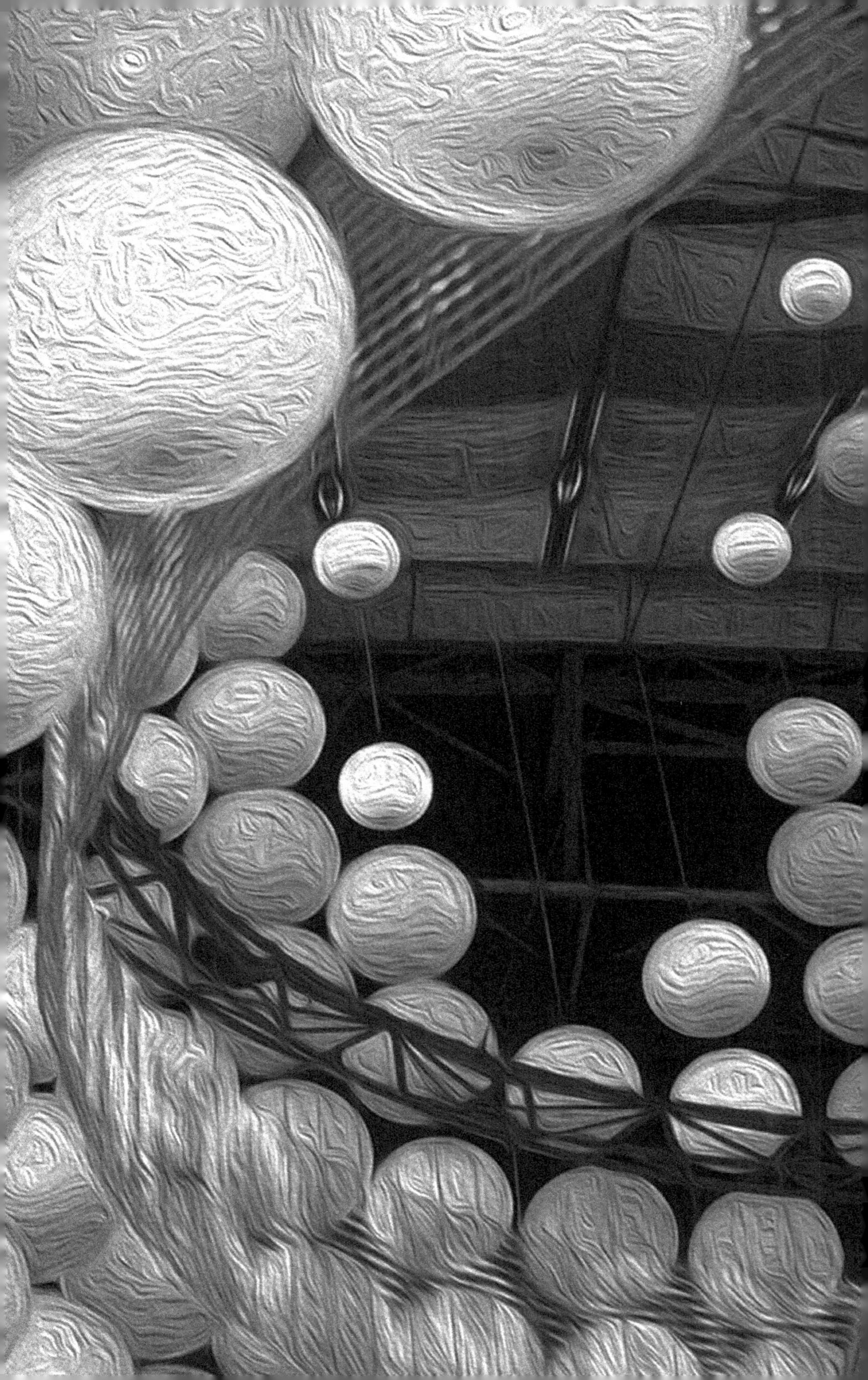

Live the Moment

Live so absolutely
So completely immersed
In the present

Be so fulfilled
And enraptured
In this moment

That there is no space
To regret the past
Or fear the future

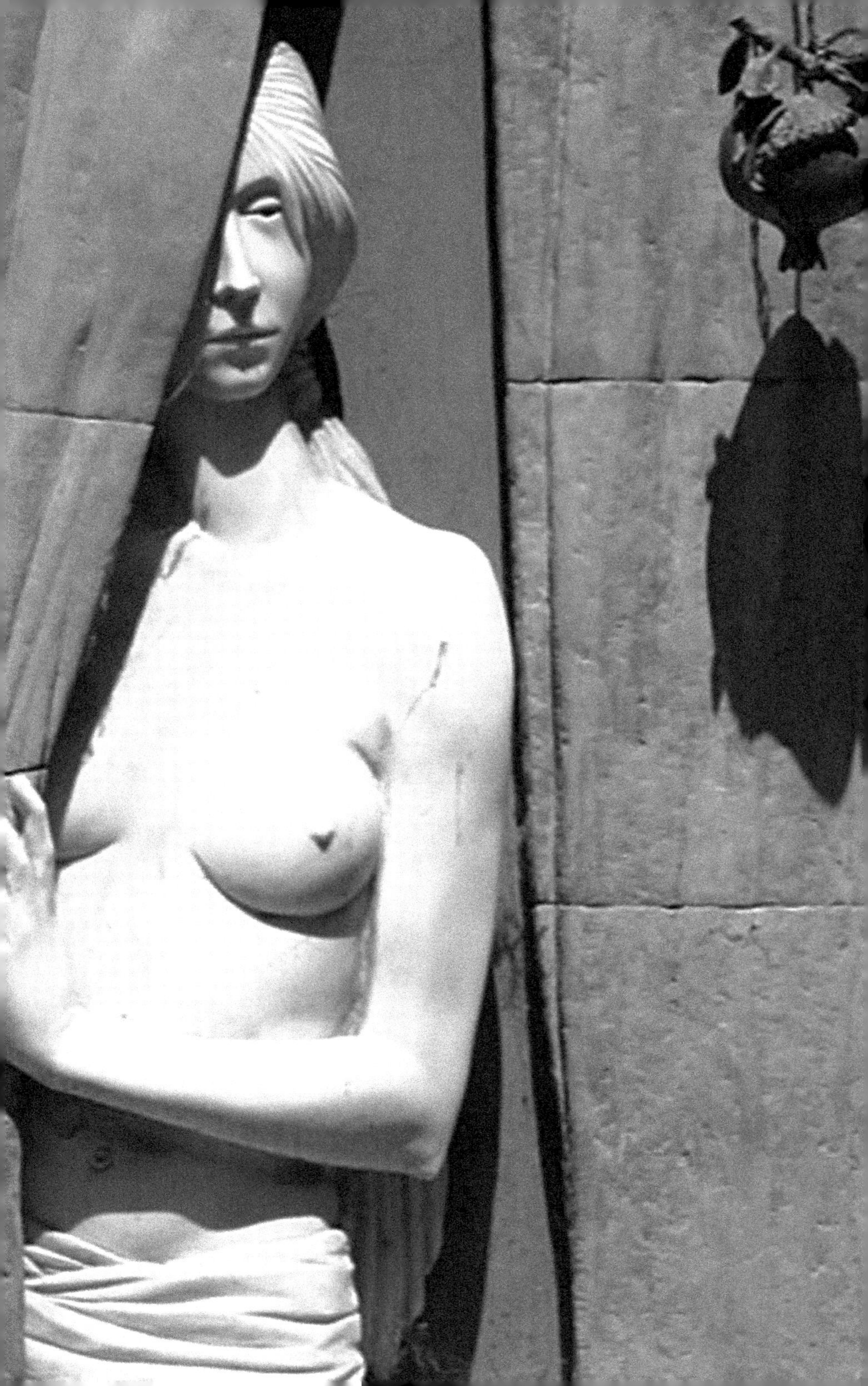

Don't be a Spectator

Do not be a spectator
Embrace the uncertainty

Know life so fully
That all doubt is dispelled

Participate without reserve
And rejoice in the knowledge
That you have tasted
Its wonders

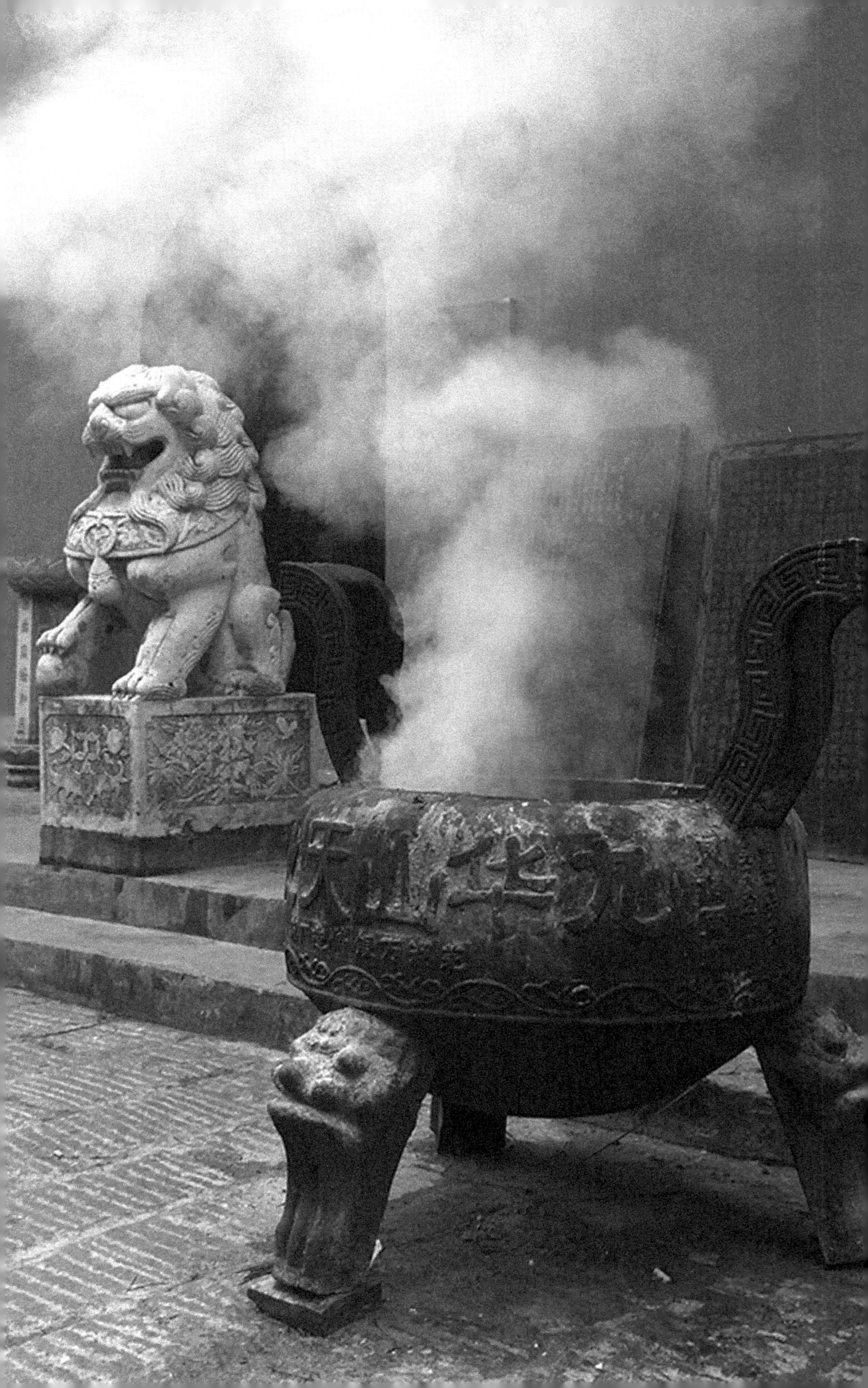

Lessons in Love

Patiently,
You taught me
That I was beautiful,
Body and soul.

Gently,
You showed me
That I was worthy,
Of love and adoration.

Esctatically,
You made me yours,
Loved me whole,
And I was lost forever.

Open Heart

The open hand

And the open heart

Are never empty

Today

There is no tomorrow

It is always today

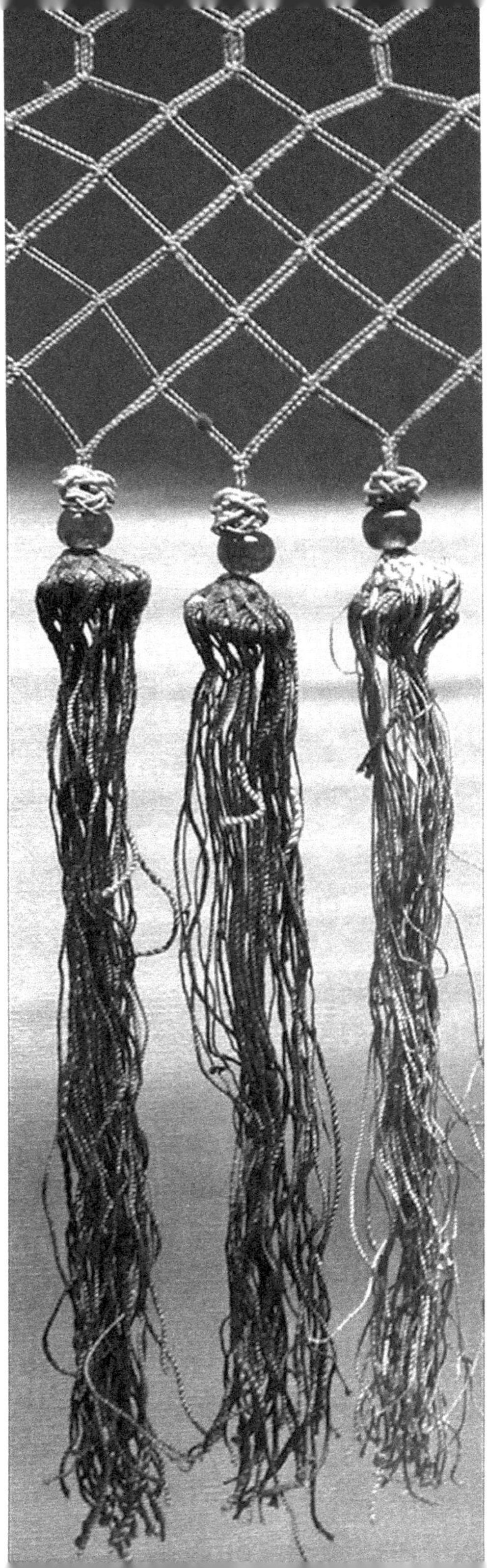

Problems

There are problems in life
That are meaningless,
Insignificant distractions
Which fill your days
And haunt your nights

Then there are problems
That lead nowhere,
Keeping you mired
In the same tired old cycles
Of want, desire and regret

Finally, there are problems
That challenge and inspire,
They lead you to learning,
A new understanding
And a higher awareness

Cherish your problems
They have much to teach you.

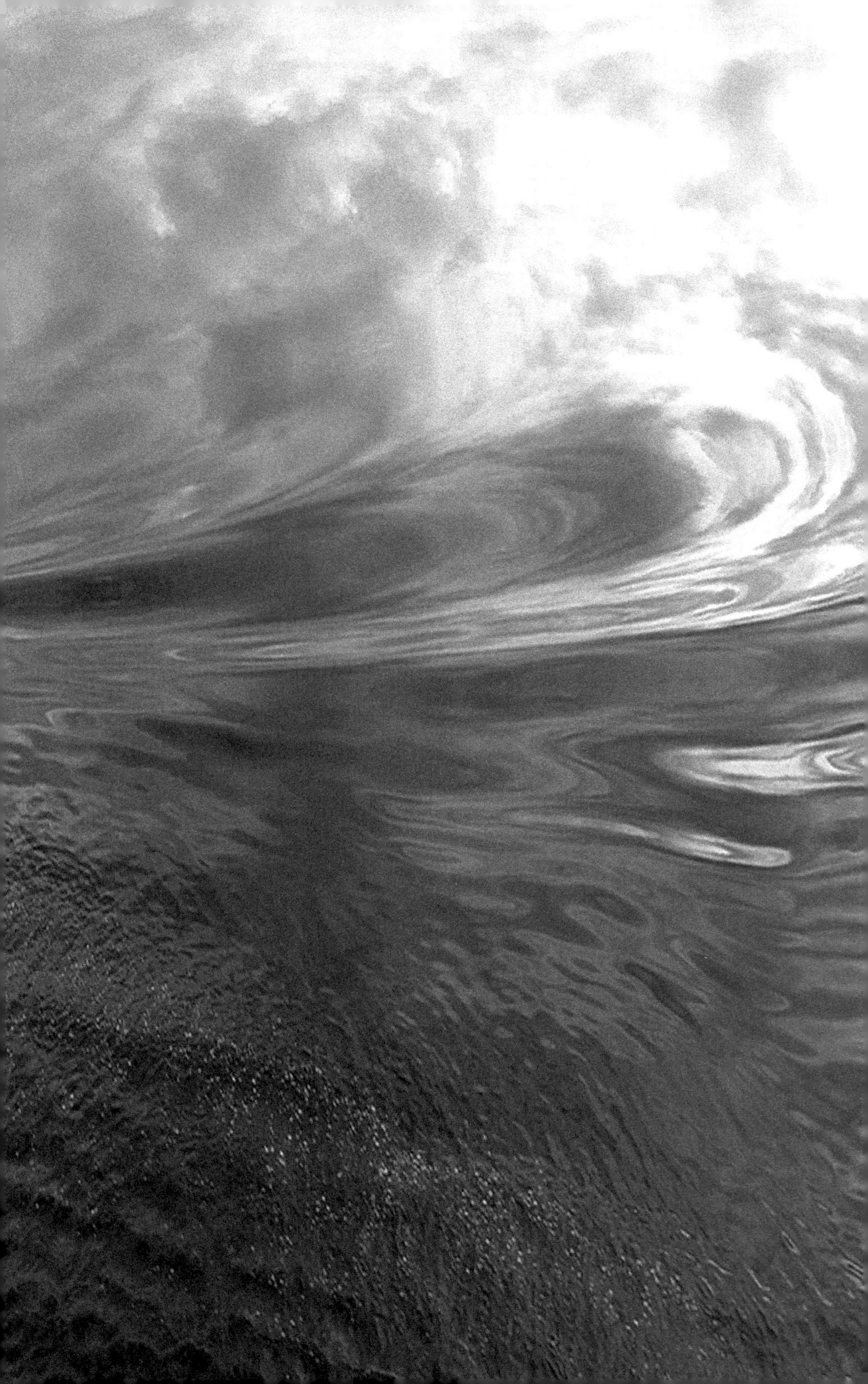

Celebrate Life

Run – with abandon
Swim – in the waters of life
Dance – to the song in your heart
Breathe – and hear the whole world
Resonate in unison

For you are alive
And that in itself
Is worthy of celebration

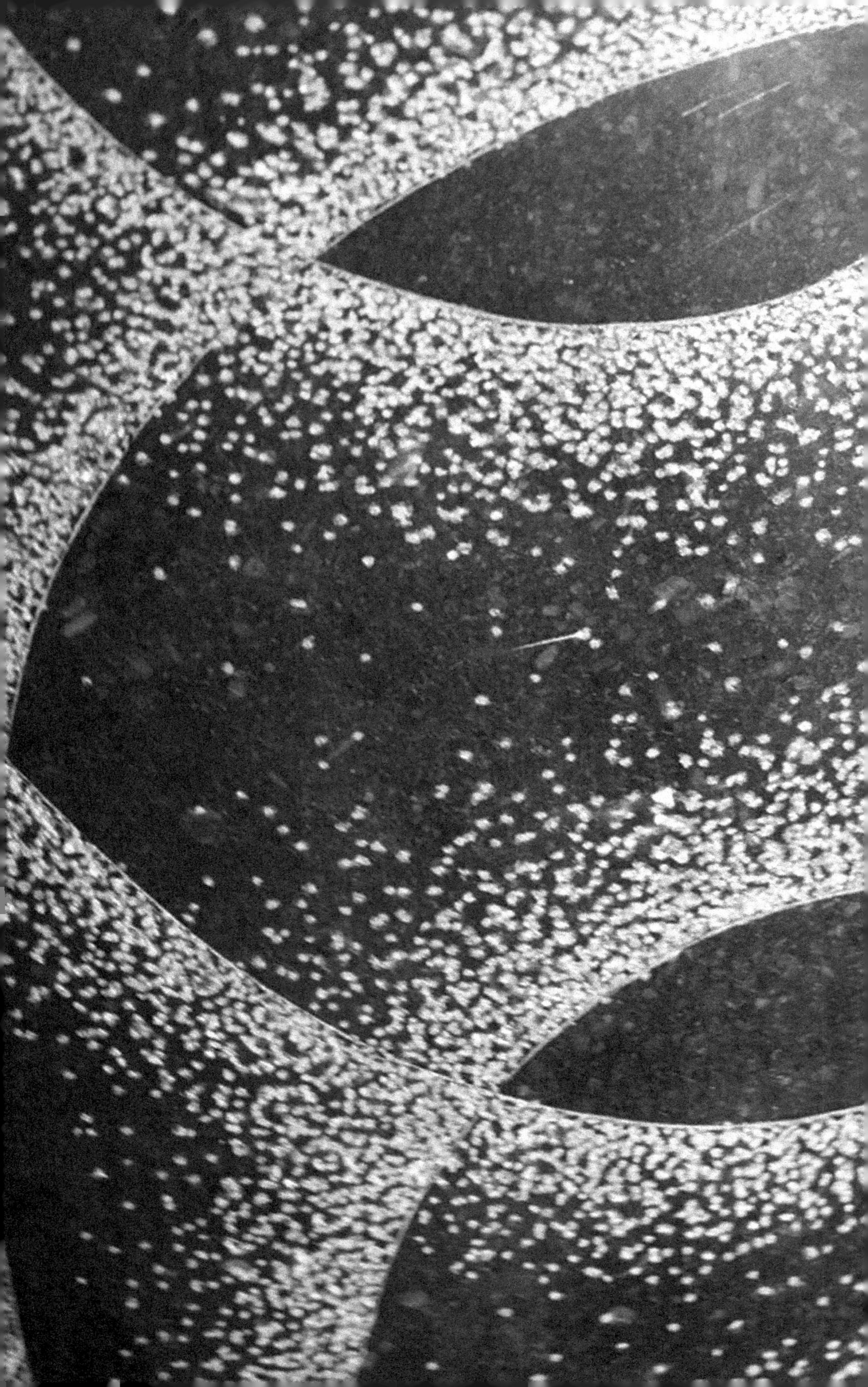

Precious Moments

Make time

And space

In your life

To live!

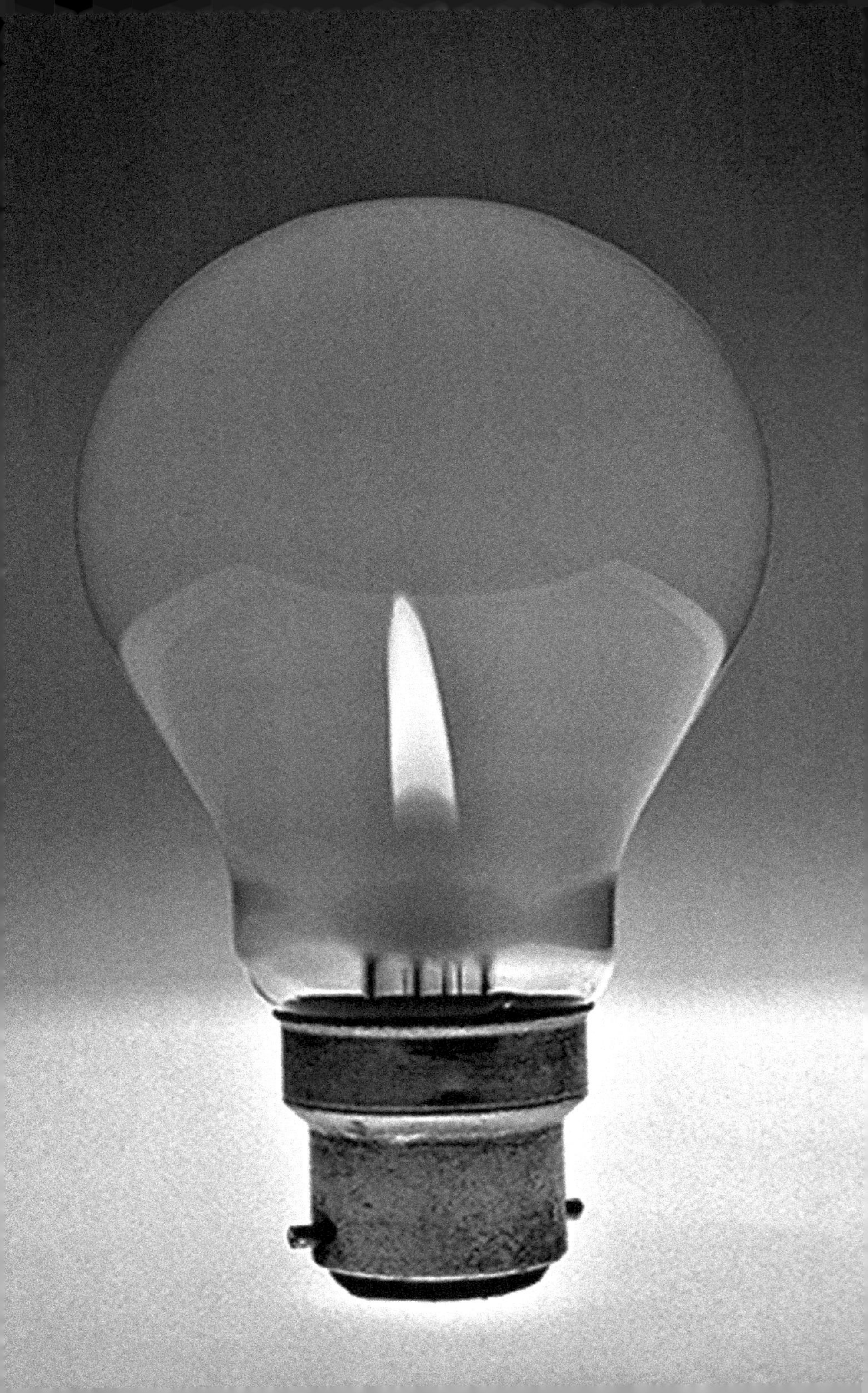

Find your Way

Stop looking *out there*
For answers
The answers are not *out there*

They cannot be bought
Nor given or exchanged
But granted by experience alone

They are *in here*

The way *is inside*

Find your way

Life is a Miracle

Life may be messy

It can be complicated
Or utterly confusing

But ultimately
It is a miracle

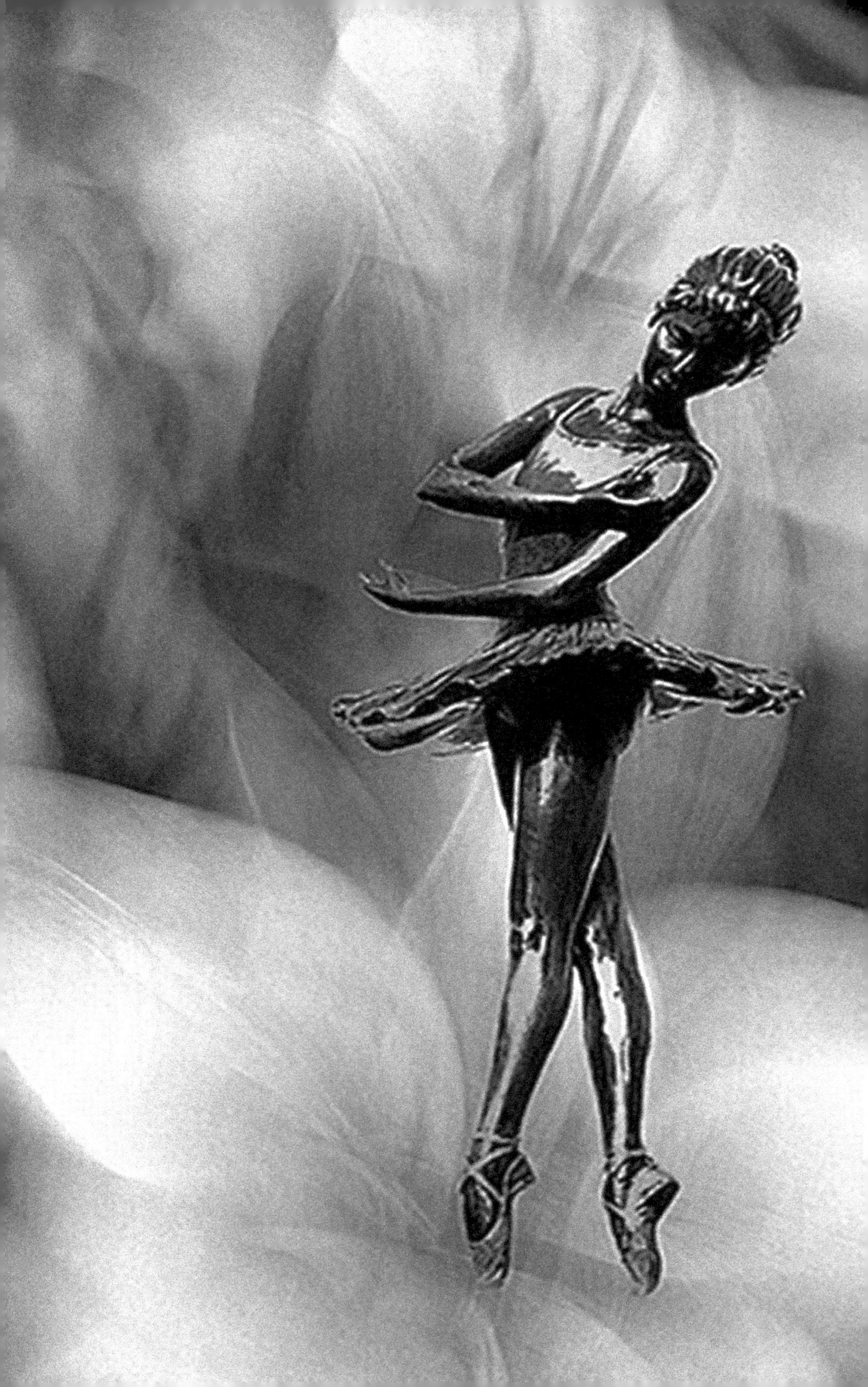

Dancing in the Flames

You and I
Little friend
Are fated
To burn incandescent
And reckless
With our passion
For life
And love

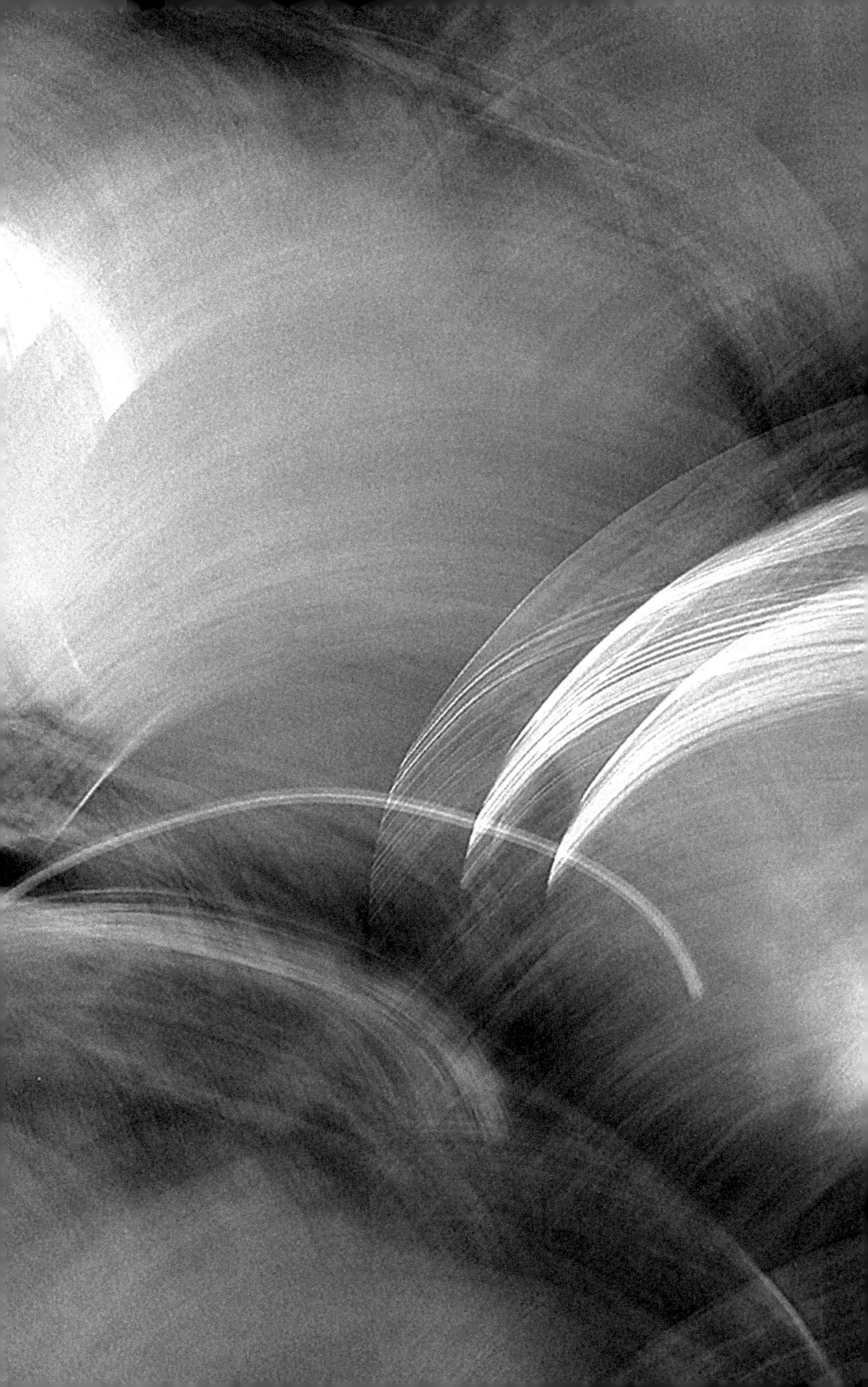

Universe

I have a universe
Within me
And the echoes of it
Shatter my fragile heart
To deliverance

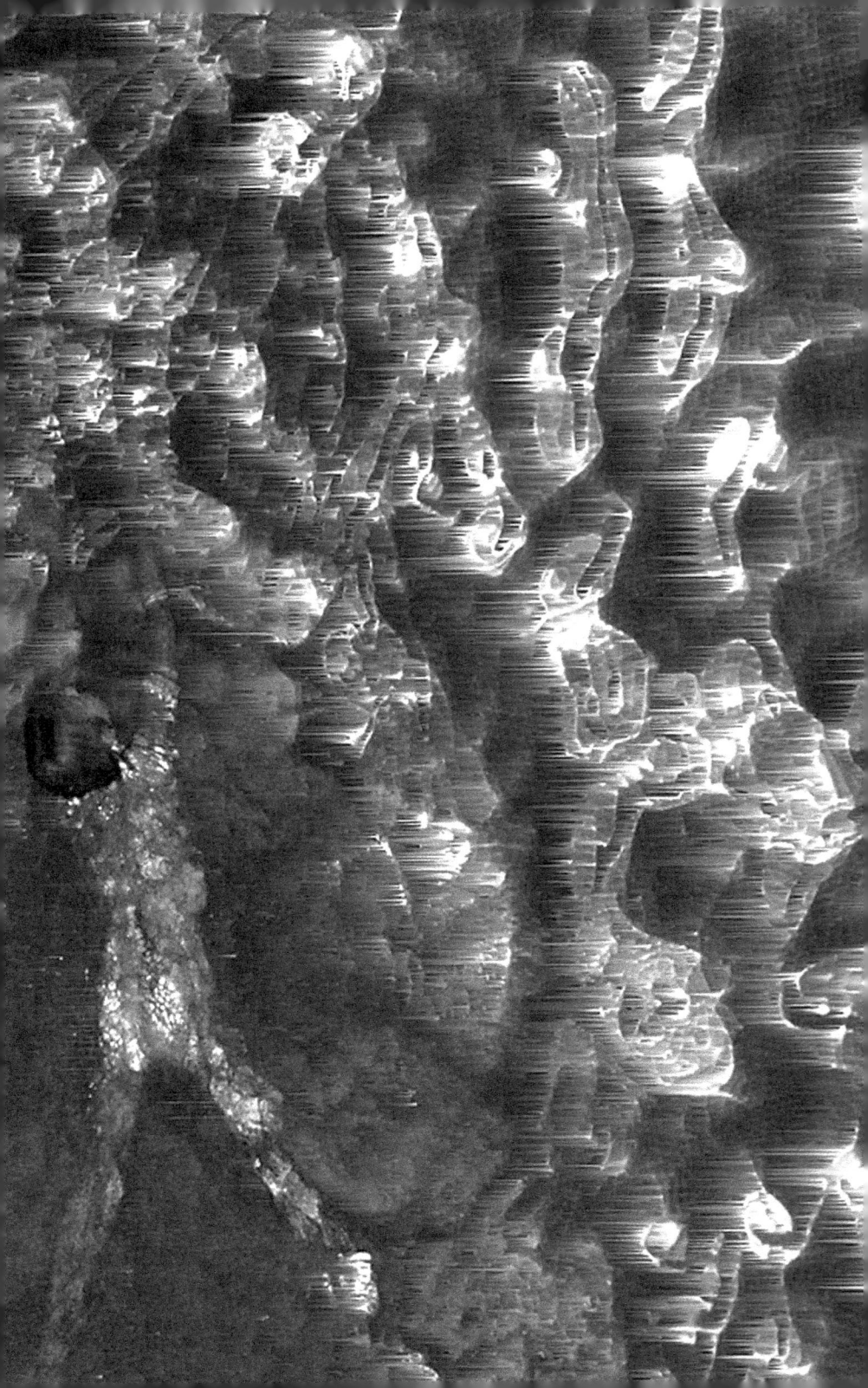

Love Knows No Bounds

Love is not bounded
By law or circumstance
It pays no heed
To age or orientation

It is as inconstant
And incandescent
As the Northern Lights

And who does not wish
To be bathed
In their mystical light

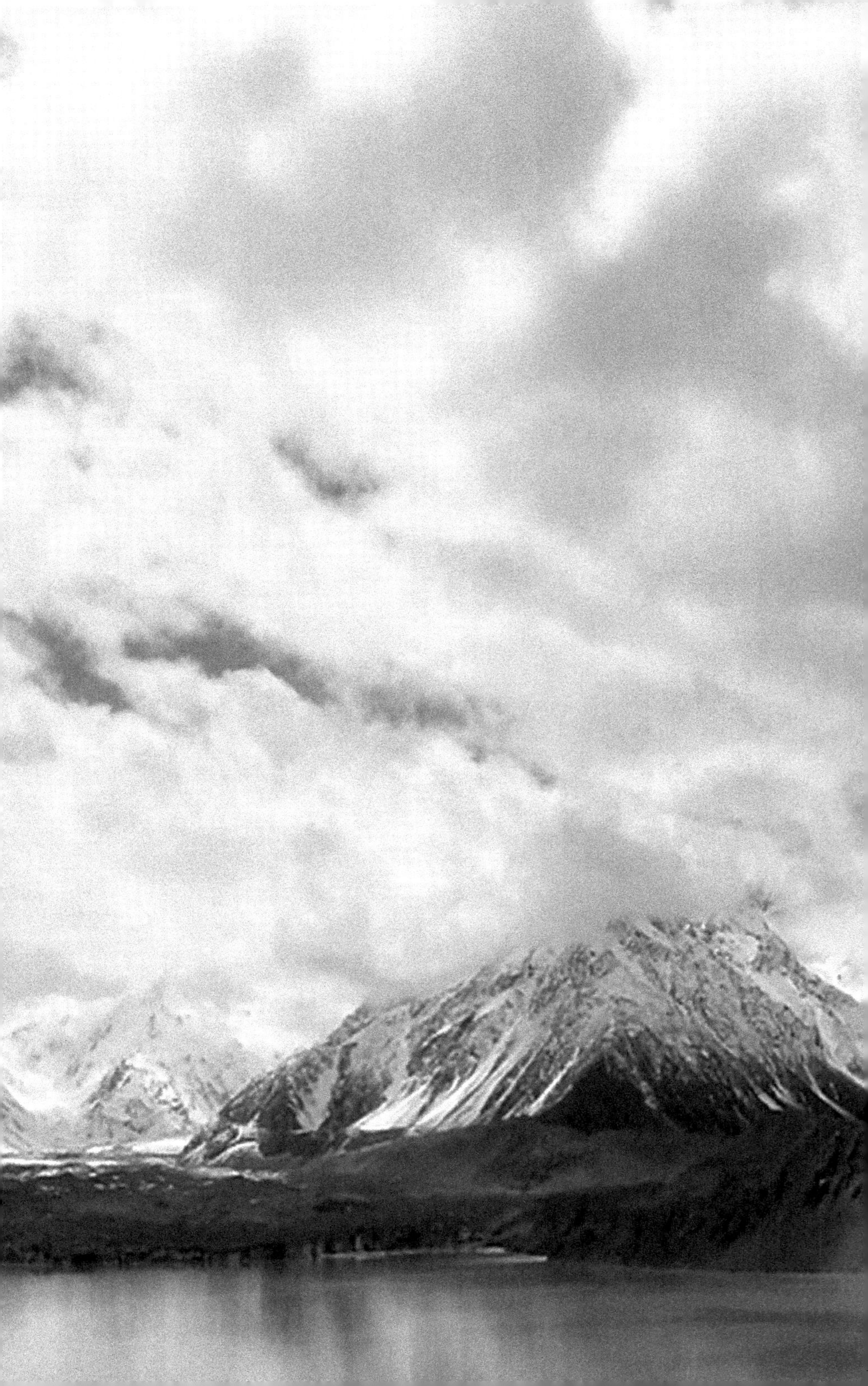

The Journey is Yours

There are many

Tortuous and varied paths

To the top of any mountain

But the only one

That will get you there

Is your own

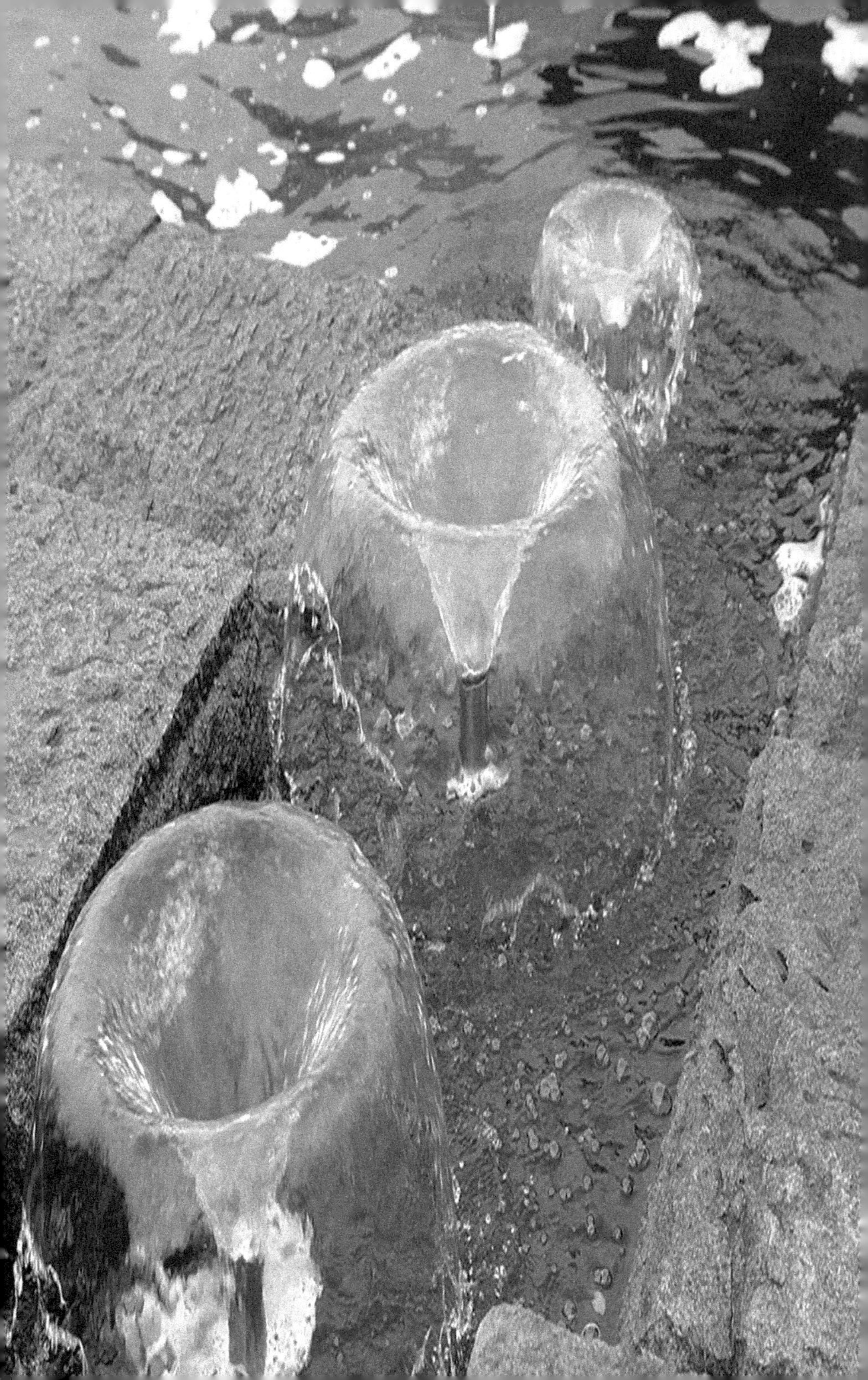

Exultation

Immerse yourself
So completely
In the waters
And ways of life
That sky and sea
Merge utterly
And every breath
Is an exultation
Wrenched from your
Unquenchable soul

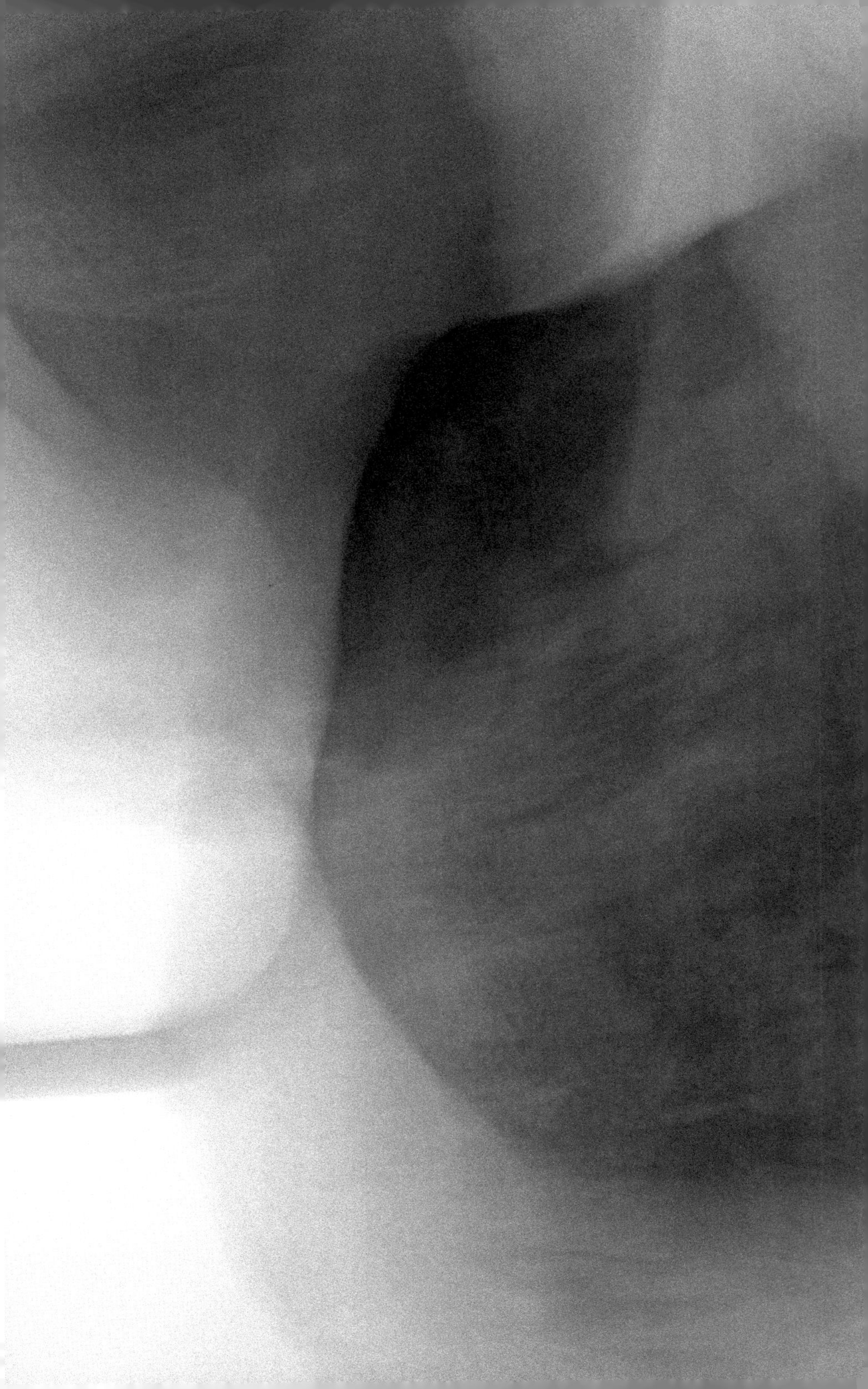

True Spirit

How you react

To the unexpected,

The unexplained

And the undesired

Reveals your true spirit

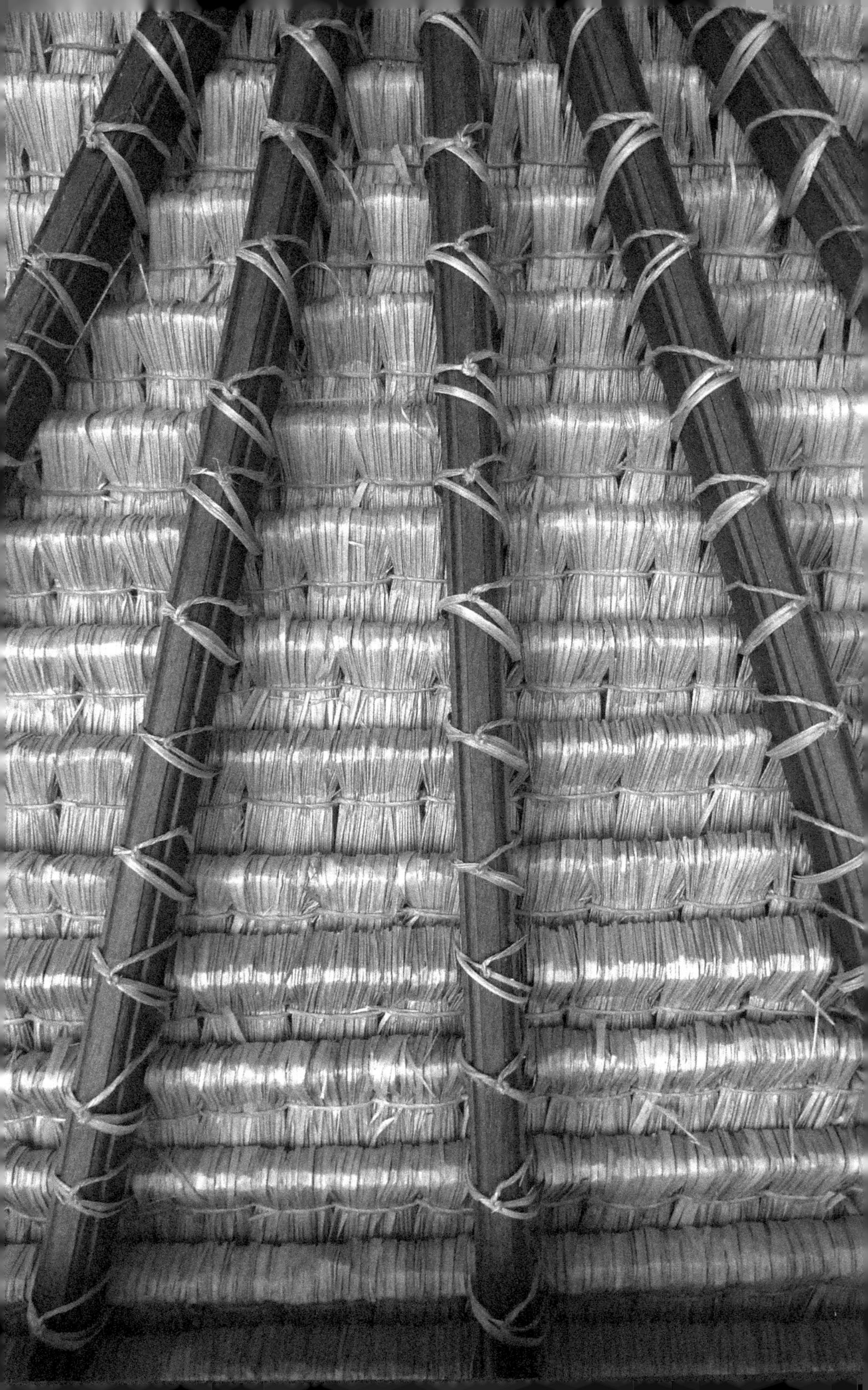

Awaken

The truth of all things
Already resides within you

You are the embodiment
Of the answer and the way

You need only awaken
To your true nature

Where sound and silence
Are one

Simplicity

Simplicity, sincerity

Passion and pride

Are the solutions

To all things

It Takes Two

Love is a paradox
It takes two
To exist
As one

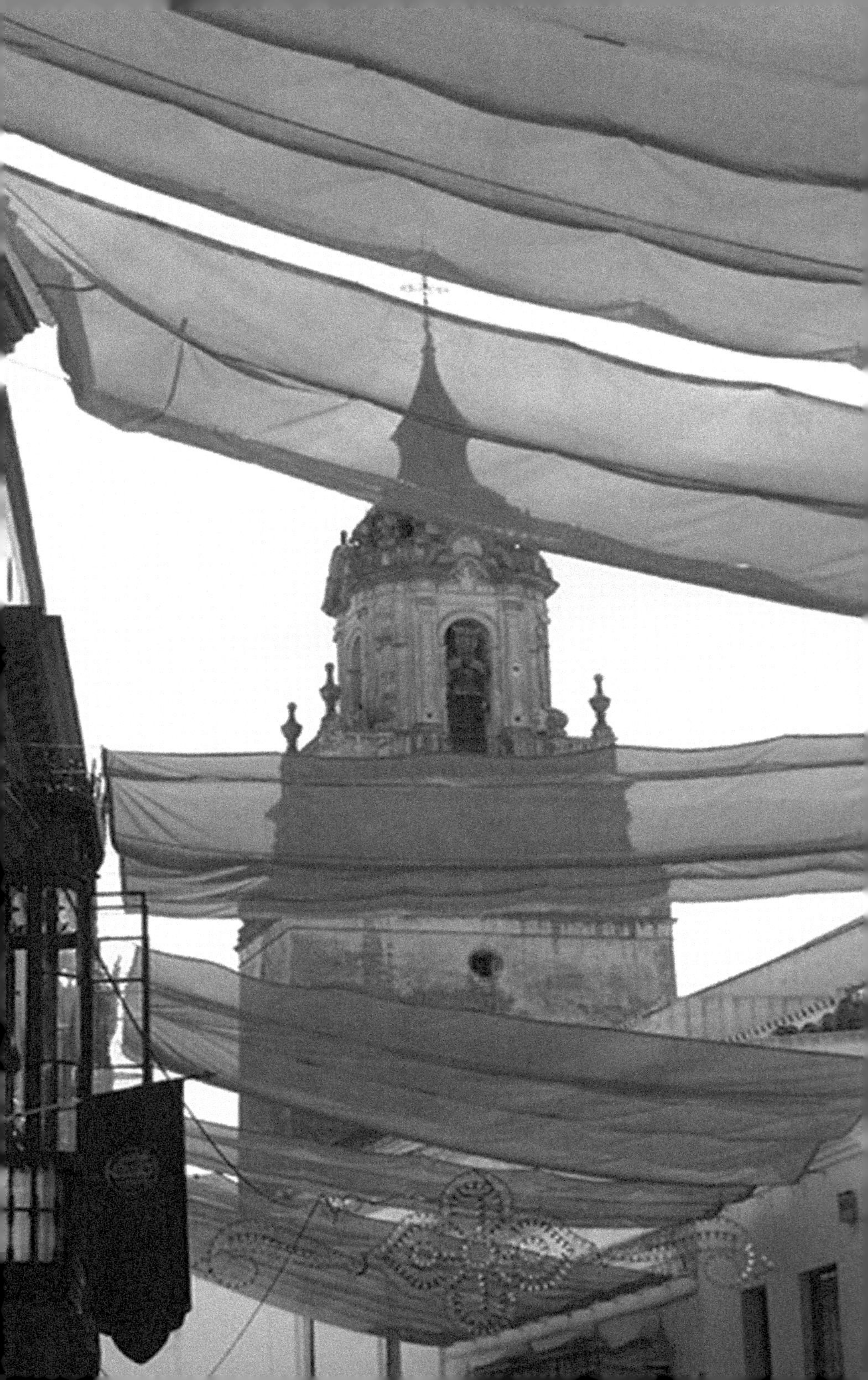

Beautiful Day

And time, like rain
Passes swiftly away
With ebb and flow
Of sea and season,
Till here, at the last
It slows and stills
In frozen recognition
Of an ending
Or beginning

And when it comes,
That final breath
Of infinite stillness,
That mortal instant
Long foretold,
Take heart,
Take heed,
For it is indeed
A beautiful day

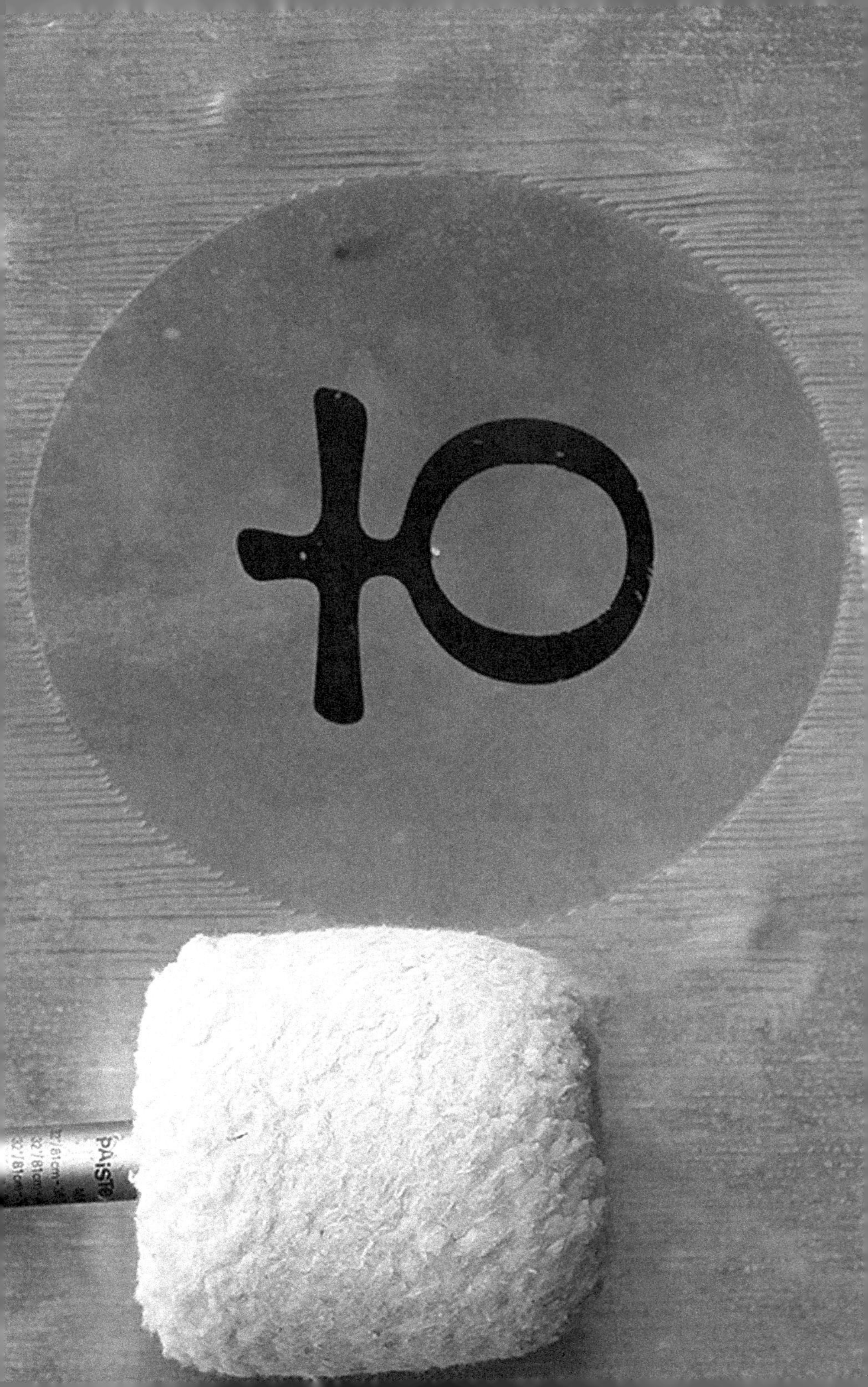

Universal Heartbeat

What is your heartbeat

If not the rhythm

Of the universe?

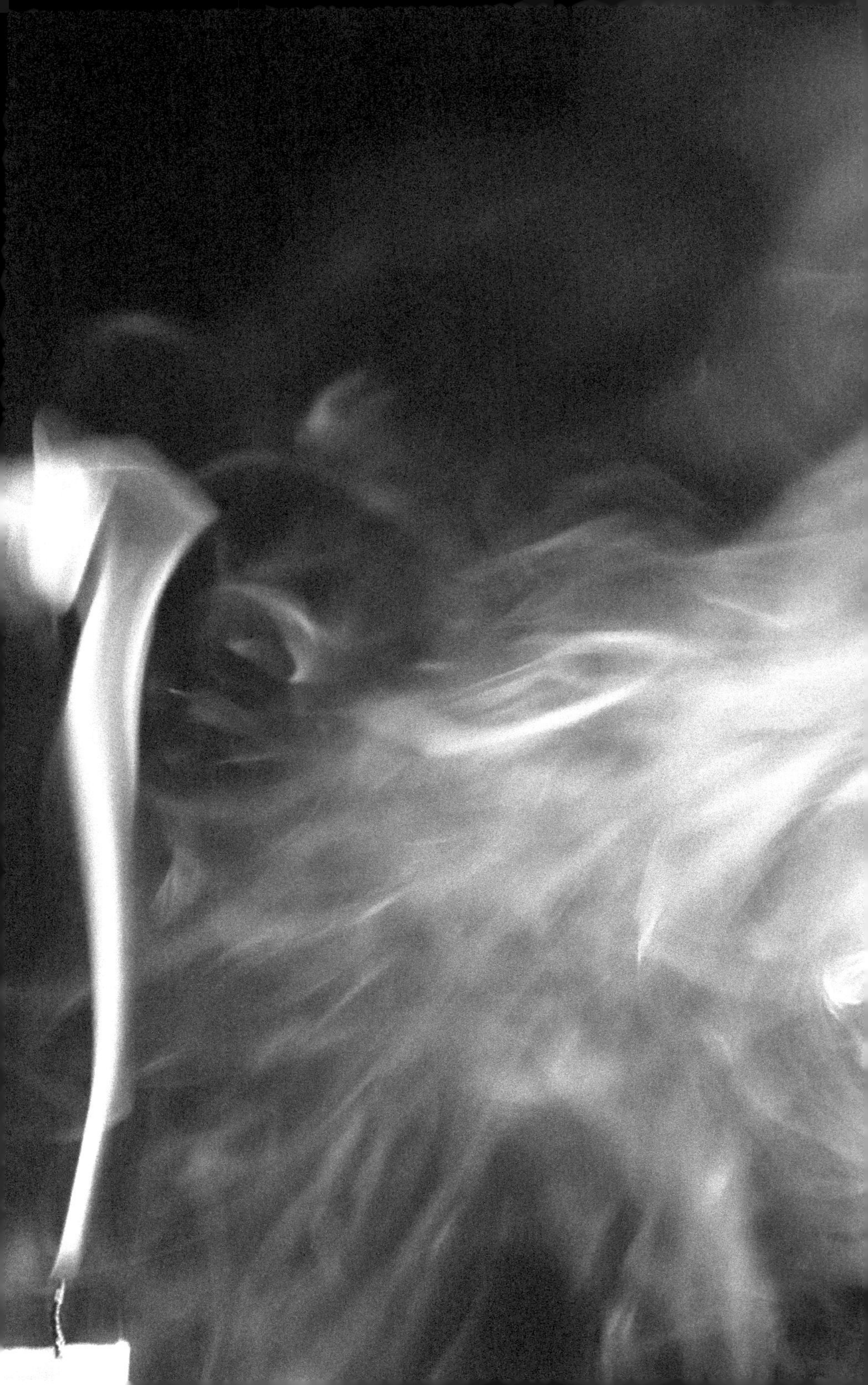

In the End

We all become memories

Make yours amazing

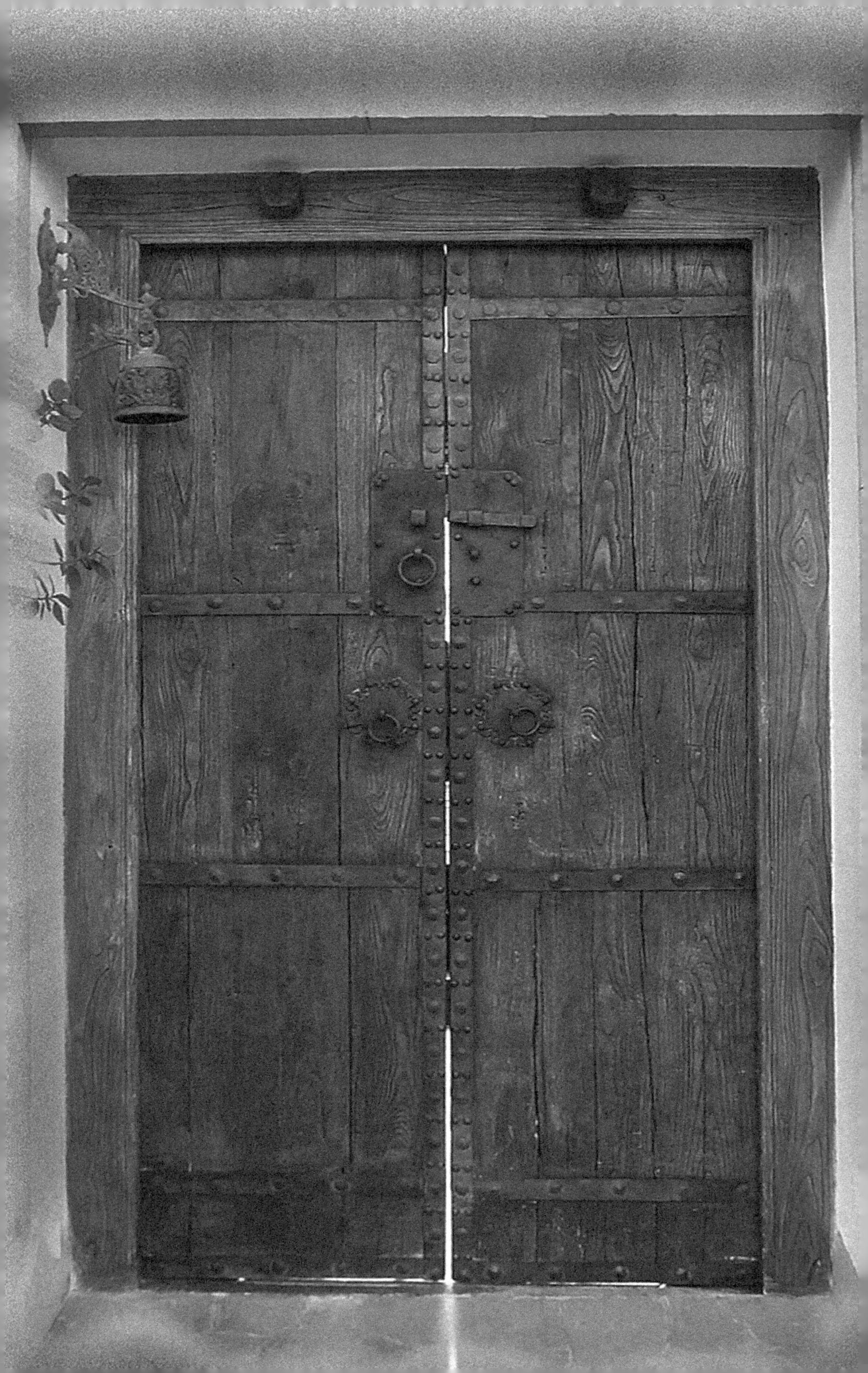

Two Become One

In these pages
We have travelled
You and I
Dear friends
But a short distance together
Seeking truth and wisdom
Along the Way
To pass through
The fire of truth
And reach the place
Where mind and body merge
And two become one

We hope that you have enjoyed
Sharing this journey with us
We thank you
For your companionship
And understanding
Along the way

Do not say farewell
For every ending
Is a new beginning
And there is no place
Where the journey ends

Dear Friend,

We thank you for your company and kindness as we have travelled the road together in these pages and hope that you have found some comfort, wisdom or understanding in them. Much as in life, none of us truly travels alone, although it can feel that way at times.

Being diagnosed with life-limiting diseases has led both us and our families to explore the depths of human resilience. None of this is possible without the love and support of others. As well as family and friends, the charities dedicated to the care and support of patients and their families have a pivotal role. Their untiring work to inform, conquer fear or stigma and to search for cures or relief is absolute. Their dedication and devotion is unmatched. The work they do is amazing. They are the gentle hand reached out in love and comfort. We are all eternally grateful to them.

The unfailing capacities of the human spirit to overcome adversity are astounding and we have learnt that life and love, dignity and dreams are worth fighting for. They are what counts in the end.

Live your dreams!

Richard & Brian

Follow the authors

You can follow us and read our stories at:

Website: www.2become1poetry.com
          www.2become1poetry.co.uk

Facebook: @2become1poetry

Twitter: @2become1poetry

Instagram: @2become1poetry

Motor Neurone Disease Association

This book has been produced in support of the Motor Neurone Disease (MND) Association. The MND Association is the only national charity in England, Wales and Northern Ireland focused on improving care and support, funding vital research and campaigning to raise awareness for people affected by MND. The charity relies on voluntary donations. Twenty-five percent of the profits raised through the sale of this book will be donated to the Association. Find out how you can get involved at www.mndassociation.org

Facebook: @mndassociation
Twitter: @mndassoc
Instagram: @mndassoc

Registered Charity number: 294354

Sarcoma UK

This book has been produced in support of Sarcoma UK, the only charity in the UK focusing on all types of sarcoma cancer. Their mission is to raise awareness of sarcoma, fund vital research into the disease, campaign for better treatments and offer support to anyone affected by sarcoma. The charity relies purely on voluntary donations to be able to do this work. Twenty-five percent of the profits raised through the sale of this book will be donated to Sarcoma UK. To find out more about sarcoma, the charity and how you can get involved, please visit www.sarcoma.org.uk

Facebook: @uk.sarcoma
Twitter: @Sarcoma_UK
Instagram: @sarcoma_uk

Registered Charity number: 1139869 England and Wales
                           SCO44260 Scotland